PaRappa the Rapper

PaRappa the Rapper
Mike Sholars

Boss Fight Books
Los Angeles, CA
bossfightbooks.com

ISBN 13: 978-1-940535-31-9
First Printing: 2023

Series Editor: Gabe Durham
Associate Editor: Michael P. Williams
Book Design by Cory Schmitz
Page Design by Christopher Moyer
Book Typesetting by HMDpublishing

This book is dedicated to my Grandmother,
Rima Banerjee.
When I was little, I wanted to be just
like you when I grew up.
Allegedly, I grew up. I still wish I was more like you.
I love you the most. I miss you even more than that.

CONTENTS

WORTH THE WAIT

WHEN I CLOSE MY eyes and focus, I can map out the exact route of my favorite childhood pilgrimage. Depending on the weather or the state of my crash-prone bike, the round trip could take an hour or more. That's a long trip when you're a kid, and I made it hundreds of times. But my efforts were always rewarded, and I rarely came back empty-handed. What is a pilgrimage, if not a journey for a greater understanding of yourself?

My childhood destinations were Blockbuster Video and the Meadowvale Library. Everything that followed in my life was built upon that.

In the fall of 1997, I was a ten-year-old living with my mom, grandma, and brother in the suburbs of Mississauga, Ontario. It's a mid-sized city that orbits the metropolis of Toronto like one of Jupiter's moons. It was diverse and Canadian enough to support my immigrant family, but the gravity of the bigger city pulled us closer.

It's weird to have dreams of moving 45 minutes east (30 if the traffic on the 401 is light), but like everyone else living in the Greater Toronto Area, we were satellites. Our suburban sprawl of a hometown revolved around a city that I rarely visited during my childhood. My mom, raising me and my little brother after jumping from India to London to America to Single Parenthood, would ride a train into the mouth of Toronto every morning, and come back in the evening, exhausted. And then she had to deal with us, her mixed-race kids, brimming with chaotic and clinically-diagnosed ADHD energy.

My brother and I were exhausting then, and we're probably just as exhausting now. Every immigrant parent is a fatalistic survivalist: They've been dealt some of the shittiest hands life can deal out, and yet continue to get the job done. Millions of kids like my brother and me were raised by their own diaspora-laden versions of Sarah Connor or Rick Grimes, parents ferrying us through the post-apocalypse of leaving their home behind for the unpromised potential of a new one.

Both of the women who raised us worked full time, and only now as a working adult do I appreciate how horrifying that must have been. I cannot imagine coming home after a long day of bullshit to deal with my anxious, loud, really-wanting-to-talk-about-dinosaurs childhood self. Later in my life, Mom told me how our family was essentially banned from our local grocery store because of the destruction my brother and I left in our wake every Friday night during her weekly food run.[1]

Every Friday became a tense negotiation between a pair of exhausted working women and their sons, who could only show love through screaming. A budget-friendly distraction was required, and that's where Blockbuster Video came into play.

I cannot overstate the importance of Blockbuster in my life, at the risk of sounding like the Ghost of Physical Media Past. Video games ensnared us early, if somewhat coincidentally. My brother and I got our first console, the Super Nintendo, for Christmas in 1993, because our Mom saw a newspaper article about it.[2] *Super Mario World* was our introduction to an entire medium that has since nourished, challenged, and grown alongside us. As the only local Black/Brown kids for huge swaths of our developmental years, we got from games the tools to relate to other kids without focusing on our differences. Gaming showed up when we needed it most, right before our parents split up, and became the central distraction we'd bond over for the rest of our lives.

1   We had been Mario Kart fans since the Super Nintendo. We had access to shopping carts. The rest is a foregone conclusion.

2   Other things I received because of newspapers: a 2nd-generation Tamagotchi (1997), *The Legend of Zelda: Ocarina of Time* (1998), my career in journalism (2007-20XX).

But games are not cheap, especially on the wrong side of a Canadian exchange rate. We only received video games as birthday and Christmas presents, so Friday night Blockbuster rentals at Meadowvale Town Centre became our way to play something other than the well-loved library of games we owned. Choosing the right game was an exercise in brotherly diplomacy and negotiation, balancing his love of two-player games with my love of single-player games (that he watched me play). We enjoyed hundreds of games over the years, across every console, until Blockbuster finally went bankrupt.

The hobby was cheaper when you could pay under $10 to take home the newest title, but you needed patience and luck: Each Blockbuster stocked different games, and their rivals at Rogers Video (or Hollywood Video if you're nasty) often carried entirely different selections.[3]

There is no equivalent to Blockbuster now. Game sales come and go, especially for digital titles (with their uncertain ownership and future-proofing), but, outside of relatively new services like Microsoft's Game Pass and Sony's PlayStation Plus Premium, there is no easy way for a kid to play a brand new game for anything less than full price. Hell, with physical media being treated

3   We could only rent *EarthBound* at Rogers, for example. And because I found the game obtuse and hard to follow, I mostly spent my time sniffing the trading cards that came with the Player's Guide.

as a luxury add-on with each subsequent console generation, that hypothetical kid can't even borrow that new game from a friend after they're done.

But in 2022, maybe that hypothetical kid doesn't even exist. The most popular games in the world are free, or offer free-to-play versions. Those same games can be accessed on every console, laptop, tablet, or phone made within the last decade. Ownership, physical or otherwise, is a rapidly-deteriorating concept. But accessibility to the art form has never been more prevalent. My childhood, like a lot of my formative years, was caught between two eras of an art form in flux.

Would I have loved games as much if I could have only played a new one every six months or so? What happens to a palette if it can't expand? Where could that curiosity have gone without rentals, or borrowing from friends, or getting free demo discs from magazines?

In the fall of 1997, those sources were my lifeline to a passion I'd have otherwise been priced out of entirely. I don't know what interests I'd have pursued, or perspectives I'd have fostered, if I didn't have an affordable entry into gaming.

But I know one thing for damn sure: I never would have discovered *PaRappa the Rapper*.

THE HIP HOP HERO

THE FIRST HURDLE TO me ever playing *PaRappa* was a big one: My family didn't own a PlayStation (PS1). But my best friend Sean did. Sean's family was straight out of a TGIF sitcom: a nuclear unit of unfailingly nice White people with a dad, mom, son, and daughter. Sean's mom made me orange peel candies when I was sick. His dad took me along on camping trips to give my life some semblance of a positive male figure, and to help me realize that real fishing was *much harder and more violent* than the minigame in *Ocarina of Time*.

Sean, a year older than me and a feature of my life until different high schools found us splitting ways, seemingly had a new console or game every time I saw him. At his house, I could *play* the games I'd otherwise only read about in magazines. Most importantly, since he was also an eldest child, sharing all his cool shit was second nature to him, and I happily took him up on it. By the time I turned ten, his family had moved out of the circle of townhouses we had lived in, and relocated a five-minute drive north.

I wasn't driving, though—I was riding. I was late to learning how to ride a bike; Sean and the other neighborhood kids taught me how to do it when I was nine, because by that point I was already taller than my five-foot mother. I rode with all the skill and care you'd expect from a child taught to drive by other children. I crashed enthusiastically and often, while somehow never really going that fast. Not accounting for collisions, it took me 30 minutes each way to get to his house and back in time for dinner.

Just like my private pilgrimage to Blockbuster and the library, this hour-long childhood trip rewarded my faith with something new—a demo of a weird and wonderful game about a rapping dog.

PaRappa the Rapper is a PS1 musical rhythm game released in North America on November 17, 1997. It's not inaccurate to say it's *the* game that confidently and joyfully invented our modern idea of the rhythm genre. When I visited Sean's house that fall, he had the *Jampack Vol. 2* demo disc loaded and ready. The Jampack series of demo discs was released by Sony as a standalone companion to their *PlayStation Underground* CD-ROM magazine. They typically sold for five to ten dollars Canadian, and represent the high-water mark of brands convincing minors to pay for a collection of ads and propaganda.[4]

The *Jampack* demo disc is, to put it charitably, 90s as fuck. The main menu is a 4x3 grid of blurry video thumbnails playing simultaneously, waiting for your brightly-colored cursor to choose among them. A constant loop of inexplicably hardcore heavy metal riffs plays in the background as you waver between *Cool Boarders 2, Tomb Raider 2, Intelligent Qube,* and *Fighting Force.* Eventually you will pick them all.

A childhood spent in Blockbuster's carpeted aisles had taught me to love the act of browsing: When you can only rent one thing, looking around and choosing properly becomes an important part of the process. Demo discs punched me right in the buffet-loving, window-shopping pleasure center of my tiny brain.

We played *Tomb Raider 2* first, taking turns drowning and getting shot in a wine cellar a few times. Back then, Lara Croft was a stack of jagged polygons crammed into khaki shorts that magazines and cover art insisted was, in fact, a very attractive woman. By 2018's *Shadow of the Tomb Raider*, she's rendered with so much photorealistic detail that players can watch her forehead wrinkle as she comprehends her own place in the history of colonialism. Her appearance in the Jampack demo disc

---

4   Or as we call the practice today, *Fortnite.*

is now more artifact than art, a faded marker on the highway of technological progress.

Then we were ready for what was to become the afternoon's main event. When you choose *PaRappa* on the Jampack menu, a splash screen shows you the controls: Kick, block, punch, chop, turn, pose. Is this a fighting game? Why is there a fighting game about rappers?

And then the title screen hits: A cartoon dog in an orange beanie, surrounded by a thick white outline as if he's still being drawn to life, jumps onstage with a mic in his hand. A DJ/teddy bear wearing shades keeps the beat going underneath him. The loading screen, with pixel text over a collage of tiny character portraits, asks for your patience: A Moment.......

It's an ongoing self-burn to look back at what we thought was the pinnacle of technology at any given slice of human experience and chuckle at how damn pleased with ourselves we used to be. In 1997, I thought *Toy Story* and *ReBoot* set the standard of computer-generated graphics in film and television. I remember a friend's dad gloating that his new PC was a Pentium II with over *three gigabytes* of storage space. It could play *Myst*, for Pete's sake! But *PaRappa* looked unlike anything I had ever seen.

In the 2020s, *PaRappa still* looks unlike anything I've seen before. I can only compare it visually to its own sequels and spinoffs, as even its 2017 remaster for the PlayStation 4 mostly just smoothed out jagged edges and kept the core art style intact. It looks, sounds, and plays like a new, strange, wondrous thing. Like you've peeked into another room and saw something that wasn't *quite* ready for the world yet; or was it the other way around?

The game starts. You are a dog in a karate dojo, standing next to an onion. The onion is wearing a blue karate *gi*; the sharp lines of his beard, mustache, nose, and eyebrows are all connected, like a calligrapher's brush stroke. His intense gaze is only slightly diminished by the visible stink lines rising above his unsprouted bulb of a head. Otherwise, it looks like the start of every *Street Fighter II* match. And then the karate-onion lets out a battle cry, his voice echoing through the room, shakes his body, and begins to fight.

And then he starts rapping.

There's no twist here, no reveal. *PaRappa the Rapper* is a music game; we know PaRappa is a rapper by the time we've finished reading the title. But, growing up with the space limitations of Nintendo cartridges, full voice acting was a rare treat. The entire demo takes three minutes to complete, as *PaRappa*'s core gameplay loop reveals itself to be a sing-song version of Simon Says with timed button presses as your only real means of control. If you time your buttons right, your score goes up by (seemingly) arbitrary amounts, and you keep rappin' GOOD according to a meter in the bottom-right quadrant of the screen. Fail (and we all failed, almost immediately) and you'll watch it drop to BAD, then AWFUL, and then the song unceremoniously ends and you're given the option to retry.

Sean and I played that single level again and again. While one of us played, the other joyfully scanned the background for visual gags. We both got good enough to finish it, but then became intrigued with the highest tier of rappin': COOL. We never did learn how to rap Cool that day. And then I went home in time for dinner, an onion man's rap lodged in my skull for the rest of my life.

I wouldn't play *PaRappa* again for three years. I was late to the real party, so let's talk about what happened in my absence.

PLAYSTATION
STARTUP NOISE

IF YOU BOOTED UP your PlayStation on any given day in November 1997, you took part in a ritual conducted by millions of others across the world. First, you released the mysteriously black-bottomed PS1 CD-ROM from its jewel case, then you popped the top of your cloud-gray PlayStation open and inserted the disc. The two-part soundscape of the PS1 boot-up sequence washed over you, as the Sony logos emerged into being on top of white, then black, backgrounds.

If your disc was scratched (or if you had a mod chip installed because *crime is cool*), waiting for the screen to turn from white to black was like watching God flip a coin. But everyone who played a PS1 game performed their own version of a start-up ritual. Playing that 16-second sound bite in public (like R&B singer/songwriter/visionary Frank Ocean did at the start of his 2012 album *Channel Orange*) is a quick way to identify Nerds of a Certain Age. Hell, my PS4 currently has a theme that mimics the PS2 boot-up sounds. Everyone's nostalgia has its own soundtrack.

After the logos and soundscapes, four unforgettable words greet you on the title screen of *PaRappa the Rapper*: The Hip Hop Hero. PaRappa stands in the middle of the screen, his paper-thin arms swinging and folding to the beat as he ushers the player to choose between "START" and "MENU." It's a high school doodle brought to life with a boombox, the perfect introduction to this game and its world.

The name "PaRappa" is a pun on Japanese words meaning "paper-thin," while also rhyming nicely with his title and profession, The Rapper.[5] Every character in *PaRappa* is presented almost as a literal translation of their hand-drawn origins, and their bodies bend, roll, and fold like paper throughout the game. While later games adopting an arts-and-crafts visual style (like *Paper Mario* on the Nintendo 64 and, much later, Sony's own *LittleBigPlanet* on the PlayStation 3) opted to focus on the paper aspect as a key part of story and gameplay, in *PaRappa*, it's just a fact of life.

Once you hit START, you get to experience the hour-long reality of actually playing *PaRappa the Rapper*. It is a slice-of-life cartoon musical rhythm game that the player experiences through six playable songs

5 "Para[para]" is the flimsy part, "rappā" is rapper. Like a bilingual onomatopoeia.

bookended by relatively lengthy cutscenes that tell the bulk of the story.

On an objective level, that's the whole game. It's absolutely more than the sum of its parts, because everything about it—the fresh art and animation style, the charming slice-of-life story, the Simon Says/proto quick-time-event gameplay loop, the amount of time dedicated to cutscenes and music videos—was nearly unprecedented at the time of its release.

Since I didn't experience *PaRappa* at launch, it's worth exploring the landscape around the time it was completed, and what fans and critics were thinking at the time. And if there was one thing I was obsessive about in 1997, it was video game criticism.

As a child, I quickly found my passions and talents through a rapid-fire process of elimination, until I was left with the combo of reading, writing, and video games. I wanted to be a video game critic for almost as long as I knew that was a job. I'd pay for my trio of magazine subscriptions with money from my allowance and haunt my public library at the end of each month to read all the others I couldn't afford.

I pored over the reviews in *Electronic Gaming Monthly (EGM)* and compared them to the ones in *GamePro*. Even back then, a video game review was already given an inflated sense of prominence. Most magazines put their review scores in the final pages of each issue; your reward for sifting through ads and fold-out posters that doubled as level walkthroughs on the other side.

But the review itself? That was *numbers*, son. That was science.

I remember seeing games dissected in no more than 300 words in a tight column; the end result of years of collaborative labor broken down in metrics like Graphics, Controls, and Sound. (Not "Music," but Sound!) This format hasn't vanished, it simply moved online and became even more lucrative for both the companies that own today's gaming news websites, and the publishers that benefit from 24/7 coverage and discussion of their products.

At its best, art criticism attempts to translate extremely subjective emotional reactions in more universal terms, even if turning feelings into numbers fails to do anything of the sort. Still, many fans want that analysis communicated through a ten-point scale; more akin to something out of *Consumer Reports* than Roger Ebert. This struggle is still felt today, but at the time of *PaRappa*'s release, numbers ruled the day.

James Mielke's reviews in *EGM* could always distill a piece of interactive art down to a paragraph and a point total; he was one of the first game critics I knew by name. As both a DJ and a seasoned veteran of both games journalism and development, he was well-versed in the culture around *PaRappa*'s initial release.

"*PaRappa* was a standout because it was so crisp—it was so clean," he told me during a video call. "And the closest hip hop analogy I can make with *PaRappa* is that it was the [1989 debut album from De La Soul] *3 Feet High and Rising* of video games, right? Because it's got that DAISY Age vibe."

According to Mielke, *PaRappa* "came out when Sony didn't honestly know what they were doing. So [game developers] could get away with a lot. [They] could be experimental," he says.

According to many in the game industry, the PS1 era was a wild west of new and strange games getting published as Sony tried to establish a toehold against Sega and Nintendo.

In this way, Mielke says that the novelty of *PaRappa* helped it to succeed. "What's interesting to me about *PaRappa the Rapper* is that… I don't think that it's the best game," he admits. "And the reason for that is the time and the technology." As a pioneer in its genre, *PaRappa* has its share of technical and gameplay wrinkles that made it hard for some players to appreciate it at launch.

Reviews at the time seemed genuinely vexed on how to rate (or even define) the moment-to-moment gameplay. *GameSpot* wrote that "while the gameplay is original, it's not going to win awards from fans of intense fighting and first-person racing games."

PlayStation Magazine was similarly concerned with getting the average gamer to even give the game a try. "Trying to convince many of today's action-hungry gamers to invest in a game that stars a cartoon dog who raps against an onion, a moose, a frog, and a chicken is a pretty hard sell. It ain't no picnic to describe the gameplay, either. Still, we'll give it a try: it's a kind of memory game, only with the added element of rhythm."

My personal favorite excerpt is from *GamePro* writer Scary Larry, who opened his review as follows: "At first, PaRappa the Rappa [sic] looks like a kid's game with awful graphics and stupid tunes." They should have sent a poet; instead, they sent Scary Larry.

Yet none of those technical or design shortcomings stopped those reviewers from ultimately praising the game thanks to its greatest, most enduring strength—its charming, earnest presentation. According to Mielke, those qualities helped it stand the test of time.

"It still remains a highly influential game, because people reference it all the time. *PaRappa* is iconic," he says. "It was a whole vibe in one package. There was no DLC, there were no microtransactions, there was no add on content…They were telling us the story, and you played the game based on those mechanics; you want to see it through."

If we're to apply the standards of today to the environment around *PaRappa*'s release, I find myself immediately wondering how open audiences were to a full price game of this brevity being sold alongside much lengthier games. For example, my most recent playthrough of the game clocked in at just under 45 minutes. *Final Fantasy VII*, which was released for the PS1 just two months before *PaRappa* launched, has an average play time of 76 hours and 3 minutes (according to GameLengths.com) across three discs. Both games were sold for the same price.

I don't take any issue with *PaRappa*'s playtime, nor was its length controversial at the time. As of 2004, the original PS1 releases of the game sold 1.4 million copies. In 1998, it won a Platinum Playstation Award, denoting 1 million units sold to date in Japan alone. No one was being fooled or walking away upset; or if they were, it didn't really seem to affect the game's reception. Its technical shortcomings were typical for games of its era. It was, by all accounts, a popular, well-received, hour-long, full-priced video game that received both a spinoff (*Um Jammer Lammy*) in 1999 and a PlayStation 2 sequel (*PaRappa the Rapper 2*) in 2001.

When you find an experience you love, can anyone convince you to feel otherwise? Through the eyes of an admirer, aren't flaws just downgraded to quirks? Because in late 2000, when I eventually played the full version of *PaRappa the Rapper* at age thirteen, it changed me. I saw something that my near-decade of gaming obsession had never been able to show me.

I saw myself.

•

Here's what it feels like when you can't see yourself in the things you love. I first got hints of the feeling as childhood Halloween costumes became teenage Halloween *outfits*. I always had to go a step further to find a character who looked like me. None of my favorite movies, books, and games had a single character like me, my brother, or my parents. It seemed for a while like a problem of scale; you just need to see/play/read more things. So you do. And then you run into the next phase: What happens when you see characters who *do* look like you and they still feel unrecognizable?

I am a 90s kid born in 1987, and an early conscript into the Console Wars. I found my love of music in the epicenter of a North American cultural meltdown around hip hop, or as it was called at the time: *gangsta rap*. I saw onscreen Black People; they were usually rappers, athletes, or some screenwriter's idea of the two. I saw Black stories on screen; they were usually about Black struggle or violence in a way that (when they were written by Black people) felt sincere and important, but not recognizable to me as a child of the suburbs. I was a chubby bespectacled mixed-race kid raised by his Indian mom and grandma. If someone was telling my stories, I couldn't find them. When you're told, repeatedly, that your life should be defined by trauma, anything else can feel alienating.

At a certain point, you wonder if there's a *reason* no one like you exists in the stories you love. When you meet Barret Wallace with his gun-arm in *Final Fantasy VII*, you're unaware that he'll become the standard counterpoint used against you whenever you bring up the lack of diversity in games for *decades* to come. You become so starved for fleeting moments of validation on screen that you latch onto side characters that remind you of yourself (if you tilt your head and blur your eyes). You accept the characters you're given, no matter how flat or broadly-sketched they may be.

You'll eventually gain another power to compensate: You'll get so tired of watching for Black and Brown lives in your favorite things that you'll simply look beyond color or species into Sonic's Echidnas and Disney's Goofs. You see yourself where you need to. It's either that or accept the vampire-reflection nature of the world at large; you know that you have a body, but you're unable to see it in the culture around you. But even then, it's so rare to find a mix of dignity and joy in characters you relate to. After a while you wonder if emotional depth is just a quality that you simply shouldn't be expected to possess.

And then one day a dog in a hat teaches you to believe in yourself.

A GAME MADE
BY ARTISTS

PaRappa wasn't designed to be merely the star of a single game. He was supposed to be an enduring mascot: no less than Sony's answer to Mario and Sonic, according to the man who created him, Rodney Alan Greenblat.

When Greenblat was first brought on board in 1994 to work on what eventually became *PaRappa the Rapper*, he was already working with Sony Creative Products, a licensing company within Sony Music Japan. Greenblat's distinctive style had won him an enthusiastic following in Japan, and one of his projects—a 1992 children's CD-ROM game called *Dazzeloids* that had been localized for Japanese audiences—had demonstrated his willingness and ability to translate his style to digital media.

When I talked with Greenblat, what stood out to me was his enduring interest in seeing new advances in technology as opportunities to make something different. CD-ROM and multimedia formats were in their own way, another canvas.

Born in California in 1960, he was already a celebrated multidisciplinary artist and a fixture of New York's East Village art scene in the 1980s. In the latter part of the decade, he found himself playing around with an Apple Macintosh program called Macromind Director. Through its graphics and scripting tools, he unknowingly became a pioneer in the space, leading to him being contacted by Macromind itself (which later became Macromedia, which was in turn purchased by Adobe in 2005) to help him create even more projects on their platform.

Greenblat was already well into a career as an artist working across various media—sculpture, paintings, and more—but this early rise to prominence in the relatively niche space of CD-ROM–based media in the early 1990s drew him into the orbit of an agent that ultimately made the introduction to Sony, which brought him to Japan.

His work with Sony Creative had him creating original characters to decorate physical products—like how Hello Kitty and her friends adorn Sanrio products. Sony put out a popular line of products featuring characters of Greenblat's design: the lethargic brown bear PJ Berri, hip blue feline Katy Kat, cheerful flower girl

Sunny Funny, and the sole human of the bunch, the blonde Pony Pony.[6]

Meanwhile, in another Sony office, prolific Japanese musician Masaya Matsuura was working on his first-ever game prototype, a still-untitled rhythm game built around vocal rap samples, but he lacked a visual designer. Matsuura had gained fame as leader of progressive pop/rock band, PSY·S (pronounced "Size"). Born in Tokyo in 1961, he had formed the band almost right after graduating university, finding much success in their thirteen-year, eleven-album run together. Like Greenblat, he had also adapted his art into the fledgling multimedia industry with the 1993 release of his interactive music CD-ROM, *The Seven Colors*.

A Sony Creative producer, aware that both men had expressed an interest in working on the just-announced Sony PlayStation, arranged an introduction. Matsuura, already a fan of Greenblat's work, asked him to provide character designs and art for his game. The characters he had just designed for Sony Creative made their way into this new project (except Pony Pony), but the game was still missing a main character.

"Matsuura was looking for something that would work in this kind of game idea that he had: a rhythm-chasing or, a rhythm-following game," Greenblat told me. "Rap music was perfect for that."

6 Because of her ponytail, of course. You thought she was a horse?

Since Greeblat's previously created characters were already approved by Sony, they served as a benchmark for the rest of the game's visual style.

"Sony Creative was overjoyed," Greenblat says about Matsuura's choice to integrate his three characters into the game. They had already committed to creating physical goods and merchandise featuring the trio, and now they'd be starring in a video game. But Greenblat eventually returned home to NYC, and had to contend with a new challenge: being part of a worldwide team limited by early-90s fax machines.

"I had to fax the [character] sketches to my agent, to Sony Creative, and to Sony Computer Entertainment.[7] [...] I had to write Pantone numbers where the color would be." Nineties kids might remember that faxes were black and white only. Greenblat trusted that his paint-by-numbers art wouldn't get lost in translation en route to Japan. "It was always very weird to see how the colors looked, when you actually put it together," he admits.

Every single character, background, and object that appears in *PaRappa* was designed by Rodney Greenblat, and he has the number-laden black-and-white sheets to prove it. Everything in the finished game originated in Greenblat's faxes, but some practical creative decisions

7   Which was renamed to Sony Interactive Entertainment (SIE) in 2016.

(which concepts to portray in 2D vs. 3D, for example) came from another group, NanaOn-Sha.

Founded in 1993 by Masaya Matsuura and the Japanese CG artist Kiri, NanaOn-Sha was created with the idea of making projects that combined its founders' strengths: digital music and graphics. It would soon grow into a small game development team, and their first game, *Tunin'Glue*, was released for the Bandai Pippin Atmark[8] in June of 1996. It was essentially a basic music sampling program with a cheerful, toy-like presentation. Greenblat's *Dazzeloids* would also be ported to the Atmark at the same time. Their follow-up game left more of an impact.

In a 2017 Playstation Blog interview with former Sony Interactive Entertainment President Shuhei Yoshida, Matsuura said that *PaRappa the Rapper*'s development took around two and a half years, which was considered very long at the time. By the end of it Matsuura had officially disbanded PSY·S to go all-in on games. *PaRappa*'s development was a massive case of global artistic collaboration. Gabin Itou and Ryu Watabe worked alongside Matsuura to turn the latter's samples and song demos into authentic-sounding hip hop tracks. Watabe, in particular, leaned on his

---

8 This was technically Apple's first-ever video game console. It was launched and folded in under a year, and can currently be found on eBay for an upsetting amount of money.

rap background and fluency in Japanese and English to translate Itou's original lyrics into English. The entire game is a rarity in terms of localization, having its audio performances recorded *only* in English and subtitled appropriately across all regions.

Matsuura saw the game's fate as something of a do-or-die moment for his career as a developer. "I thought to myself, if players accept *PaRappa*, then maybe I can make games for a living," he told Yoshida in that same interview. "It was the fact that players had recognized my work as an actual game that became a driver for me to enter into the gaming industry."

As a child plugged into the North American gaming news scene of the 1990s, my image of an upstart revolutionary game developer was shaped heavily by *Doom* and id Software. I devoured articles about guys like John Romero and John Carmack: influential compsci wunderkinds who deified themselves in real time. I heard Carmack was a *literal rocket scientist* and that Romero bought a *Lamborghini*.

Despite all of my favorite games at the time being designed almost exclusively by Japanese men and women, I was still picturing White guys in a dark room when I thought about how games were made. At the age of ten, I had never seen a photo of Shigeru Miyamoto or Yoko Shimomura. But I could identify Romero,

Carmack, or Will Wright in a lineup from their magazine coverage alone.

I never once considered that gaming could have room for me, because I couldn't picture it. I wasn't White, I wasn't into engineering and programming, and I didn't love heavy metal.

Learning about NanaOn-Sha, a global collective of artists doing weird dope shit, could have changed my life. What I didn't know until I began researching this book is that *every single main cast vocal performer* in *PaRappa the Rapper* is a non-White person. I'm fairly sure that's a historical first for an English-language voice cast in any video game.

But above all else, *PaRappa* was created by artists making their first game who were happy to buck the rules. As Greenblat put it, the game was "an experiment."

Yet as experimental as it was, *PaRappa the Rapper* was not the first music game.

U RAPPIN'

A DEFINITIVE WORK of art is rarely the very first example of it. Mary Shelley's *Frankenstein* is not the first science fiction novel ever written, but its influence and vision is so outsized that it's become the agreed-upon inflection point of the genre's history. Shigeru Miyamoto told Toru Iwatani, the creator of *Pac-Man*, that its sequel *Pac-Land* was a direct inspiration for *Super Mario Bros.*, but the latter is widely remembered as the first important platformer game.

The history of popular "music games" before *PaRappa the Rapper* includes the flashy-button-pressy electronic toy Simon, a warehouse full of bad pinball machines based on rock bands (and one *awesome* Iron Maiden machine), and *Revolution X*, a 1994 rail shooter where you defeat dominatrix fascists and rescue the band Aerosmith through rampant acts of domestic terrorism.[9]

So, not a lot of competition. Equally scarce was any real hip hop or rap content in gaming at all. In the days before licensed music sampling was technically feasible for most games, modern music representation was rare. But that didn't stop composers who were fans of those genres from injecting the soul of their favorite bands into their games. The bleeps and bloops of chiptune soundtracks did their best to emulate physical instruments. And for gamers in the 90s, one of the many badass things about *Doom* is how close to outright copyright oblivion the game's soundtrack drifts in its pursuit of sounding almost-but-not-quite like MIDI Metallica.

In the space of a decade, video game music had gone from a wall of noise meant to grab your attention at an arcade to instrumental tracks that felt like a real experience. Even in those early days, there were game designers that saw the potential of the medium as a place of music *creation*, as well. But no matter how quickly the technology evolved, it was still woefully ill-equipped to

---

9   The most hilarious thing about *Revolution X* is that it exists. The second most hilarious thing is that the in-game dictatorship, the New Order Nation (NON), is out to destroy all youth culture by kidnapping anyone between the ages of 13 and 30—as well as the band Aerosmith, whose members had a median age of 44 at the time.

handle the soul of hip hop: the words and language that make up a rhyme.

Hip hop music leans on the strength of lyricism more than any other genre. Every element of a hip hop track, from the time signature of its drum beat to how instruments and samples are employed throughout, is built to support and emphasize a central lyrical performance. Rappers, in turn, aren't really expected to hold a tune or adhere to any existing standards of what a vocalist should be able to do. The closest examples that predate rap as a musical technique are "patter songs," which are kind of a showoff staple of musical theater, especially in comic operas. Think of "I Am the Very Model of a Modern Major-General" from Gilbert and Sullivan's *The Pirates of the Penzance*, and you're on the right track. But patter songs are almost exclusively, joke songs.

Hip hop and rap didn't spring, fully-formed, from a block party in mid-1970s New York City. Their DNA can be clearly traced back through other Black forms of music, a.k.a. "All Forms of Music." Jazz, blues, funk soul, bluegrass, rock, and disco all found their way into the first rap albums, but the roots of rhythmic lyricism can be traced back even further. West African *griots* (a title that has meant everything from "storyteller" to "musician" depending on the time and place) would tell their stories over drum beats and percussion, giving their audience the most valuable gift of all: an oral history that they could dance to.

Hip hop as a genre, and rapping as a skill within it, cannot be unspooled from mastery of language. My favorite rappers turn spoken lines into a rollercoaster, or leave you stunned on the sidewalk as you try to process the wordplay they just slipped in between your earbuds. Are all rap lyrics dense testaments to humanity's dominion over the language it created? Nope; the library of rap verses exists across a wonderful spectrum of depth and complexity, but even at their most basic, they have the power to endure. It's how you know which maternal pasta dish rhymes with "palms are sweaty." It's why if I type out the word "Forever," you know the exact tone and cadence to repeat "Forever ever" twice afterwards. It's why the three-word phrase "I bomb atomically" prompts your brain to fill in the next several lines.

There are a number of reasons why hip hop is so underrepresented in gaming: the historical lack of diversity in the industry; the rampant fear held by game publishers of challenging the status quo. But more than any other reason, hip hop is underrepresented because it's hard to make someone feel like a rapper if they don't have the ability to rap.[10] Not that there haven't been notable attempts. I own *all of them*.

---

10   This is also what holds back all home versions of *Jeopardy!*

Get on da Mic (2004) and *Def Jam Rapstar* (2010) took the most obvious route towards emulating the experience: They turned your PS2 and PS3/Xbox 360 into hip hop karaoke machines. But once again, technology didn't really have the tools for the task. Both games essentially play like versions of Sony's popular *SingStar* karaoke franchise, where a player's syllables and pitch are registered in the game through a USB microphone peripheral. But the games can't tell if you're using the right words, the tracks are often censored down to radio edits, and the final experience feels hollow. In real life, nailing the opening verse on Lil Wayne's "A Milli" is only an achievement if you never slip, stutter, or stumble—the games never knew the difference. To this day, hip hop as an act and as a genre has yet to receive its heroic moment of in-game wish fulfillment like so many other experiences. Maybe it never will.

Masaya Matsuura was fully aware of the technical hurdles involved in making a game about rapping when he started development on *PaRappa* in 1994. He did it anyway. His solution didn't solve the rap-in-gaming riddle, but it did something arguably greater: It solved the problem of how to make music *into* a game.

•

PaRappa the Rapper's two-and-a-half year development cycle for the game began with Matsuura's desire to use voice sampling, which had become possible on the CD-ROM–based technology of the upcoming PlayStation, as a central gameplay concept. Each of *PaRappa*'s six levels unfolds the same way: Across a handful of increasingly difficult rounds (or "Lessons"), the level's AI-controlled Rap Master rhymes a single line of verse, with a corresponding series of button prompts scrolling across the top of the screen. Right after, the player (via PaRappa) needs to repeat that same line, which means pressing the designated buttons in time to the rhythm.

For example: The opening verse of Lesson 4 is as follows: *Crack crack crack / the egg / into the bowl.* But with the listed button prompts, it becomes: *Crack* [▲] *crack* [▲] *crack* [▲] */ the egg* [O] */ into the* [R] *bowl* [L]. A cursor shaped like the active character's head, moving left-to-right alongside a dotted line, serves as a general visual indicator for timing and rhythm. Your ability to hit the prompts with the proper rhythm ties directly into your Rappin' meter.

Each level of *PaRappa* ranks the player's performance across four rankings: AWFUL, BAD, GOOD, and (the elusive) COOL. Depending on how well you rap/input the correct button presses in time with the song's beat and the onscreen prompts, you're awarded or docked points. If you perform well on a verse, your score goes up and your ranking remains stable as an audio cue (a tight record scratch) plays. If you perform poorly, you lose points off your total score, a sloppier needle pull plays in the background, and the text of the next ranking down starts flashing as a warning. Two poor verses in a row drops you down a full ranking (complete with a disappointed slide whistle) on the meter, and two good verses will bump you back up.

To pass a stage, you need to finish the last verse with at least a GOOD ranking. This can lead to moments where you snatch victory from the jaws of defeat with one tight final couplet of rhymes, or choke so badly in the last verse that you have to start all over again. It's also possible to fail outright; if you drop a ranking below AWFUL, the level's Rap Master shuts down the entire production and tells you to try again.

This could come off as punitive because the core gameplay loop, especially at the time of *PaRappa*'s release, was unfamiliar and unforgiving. You have rhythm or you don't. Without the right balance of levity and kindness, even the game's candy-coated presentation could leave a bitter taste in a player's mouth. PaRappa himself sets the tone at the end of each pre-level cutscene with three words: *"I gotta believe."*

It's his catchphrase, his mantra, and the game's philosophical core, all compressed into a soundbite. If he's Rappin' GOOD or AWFUL, PaRappa isn't out here to defeat a foe or save the day; all he has to do is keep believing in himself. But in the game and in real life, that sometimes feels downright impossible.

As the game proceeds from stage to stage, each level's rhymes get more dense and unpredictable in their flow, requiring more talent and dexterity from the player. But the final, joyful moments of *PaRappa the Rapper* play identically, from a purely technical perspective, to a player's monosyllabic rhymes in the first stage.

So we have beats, rhymes, and rhythm. We have a character proudly declaring themselves to be a "rapper" on the game's front cover. There's no denying that *PaRappa the Rapper* was the first game *about* rap. But it doesn't really contain anything audiences at the time (and especially today) would see as authentic rap music.

PaRappa is a toy. It's a joyful music box full of singsong nonsense rhymes that embrace the core tools of hip hop but fail to replicate them. No hit rap song in the 90s featured endless couplets of call-and-response verses. No rapper dared to enter the studio with bars like PaRappa's: "*Step on the gas / step on the brakes / step on the brakes / step on the gas.*" Even Vanilla Ice had the wherewithal to rhyme "collaborate and listen" with "brand new invention."

That's not to say the game is an embarrassment or without any decent rhymes; far from it. Each of the four Rap Masters, the "boss rush" bathroom level, and the game-ending MC King Kong Mushi (one stage for each of them brings us to 6 stages total) bust out verses and one-liners that still shuffle their way into my thoughts to this day. Every Rap Master, from Chop Chop Master Onion to Cheap Cheap the Cooking Chicken, has rhymes and verses that speak to the lighthearted days of early hip hop—think tracks like "Rapper's Delight" by the Sugar Hill Gang and Kurtis Blow's "The Breaks," and you're in the right sonic mindset.

But PaRappa, because of his link to the player, can't ever reach those heights of lyrical free association and dexterity. His rhymes are elementary, doled out at the speed of a controller's button press. There are reasons this works on a thematic level in terms of the game's story, but for a game about rapping, you don't end up doing anything close to the real thing.

What *PaRappa the Rapper* introduced, a system where timed button presses have a direct correlation to music being played and/or performed by the player, became the *rhythm music* or *rhythm action* genre. Luminaries in that genre include Konami's *Dance Dance Revolution*, Activision's *Guitar Hero*, and the entire collected works of Harmonix (*Amplitude*, *Frequency*, *Rock Band*, *Dance Central*). That's to say nothing of more direct descendants of *PaRappa*'s playable musical: *Elite Beat Agents*, *Space Channel 5*, *Gitaroo Man*.

And while *PaRappa* represents everything we came to expect from the rhythm action genre it spawned in the years to follow, it didn't invent the wheel.

Matsuura mentioned to me that on the night before he officially began development of *PaRappa the Rapper*, a magazine editor colleague gave him a music game for PC. It used a special peripheral to let the player recreate rock songs, and he thought it was "such a boring game."

"This experience taught me what not to do," he continued. "When I think back on it now, the game I played then focused on 'competition on timing,' not 'rhythm play.' That is why it did not resonate with me."

He never named names, but I'm fairly sure that he played one of the three guitar-based games released by Virtual Music Entertainment in 1994 and 1995: *Born to Rock*, *Welcome to West Feedback*, and *Quest for Fame* (featuring the music of Aerosmith, the guys from *Revolution X*!). They were as good at predicting future trends in gaming as they were at choosing kick-ass titles for their games. As far as I can tell, these are the first rhythm games ever made.

And the games are, like Matsuura said, boring as hell. They're worth a visit if only for the FMV-drenched look into mid-90s rock, but the core gameplay of all three games made by VME boils down to strumming a plastic guitar (or a plastic pick, called the V-pick, against a tennis racket or your own leg) in time with a heart-monitor-esque scrolling line of jagged green peaks and flat valleys.

So while VME's games predate *PaRappa* and were even known to its creators, they didn't serve as an inspiration; if anything, they drove NanaOn-Sha to go their own way.[11]

The games that have followed *PaRappa* cross genres and styles. They allow for every type of musical expression. And just like *PaRappa*, they have one major thing in common.

They're nothing like the real thing.

•

I loved *Dance Dance Revolution*. I discovered it as a teenager and fell for it hard, though I was never that good at it. At my absolute teenage peak, I could clear all songs on Standard and a handful of my favorites on Heavy. Much like my approach to actual dancing, my enthusiasm made up for my lack of discipline or talent. I loved stomping on those arrows so much that I invested hours of travel time and bus tokens to visit arcades around

---

11   Virtual Music Entertainment was acquired by Namco, who released the arcade version of *Quest for Fame* in 2000; a year after Konami's *Guitar Freaks* had already made its mark. They went out of business in 2003, and the only reason that this book isn't about the Born to Rock trilogy is because I don't think we can afford the Aerosmith royalties.

Toronto, flailing in front of strangers on each venue's *DDR* machine for ten minutes before my turn was up.

While "press buttons to make dog rap" isn't the exact same experience as "stomp arrows to hear song about butterfly," Konami's entire Beatmania franchise still owes some of its success to the path that *PaRappa* blazed. The first *Beatmania* game was released in Japanese arcades at the end of December 1997, a full year after *PaRappa*'s debut. But they have vastly different goals. The Bemani games (as they are affectionately known) land somewhere between pantomime and what Masaya Matsuura described as measuring "the accuracy of player's input timing" in an email interview with me. The big Bemani games (and their American successors, *Guitar Hero* and *Rock Band*) ask you to move your body and/or manipulate a plastic recreation of a musical instrument to hit buttons in time with onscreen prompts that get increasingly frenetic as the difficulty level increases.

From a distance, it looks close enough to performance. You strum and fold your fingers over fret bars in *Guitar Freaks*, you move your legs in time to the music in *Dance Dance Revolution*, and you tell everyone around you that "this is totally how they dance in

Japan" while playing *Para Para Paradise*.[12] But for anyone familiar with the source material, it's still just an art style translated through timed button presses. They're music-based games, but they're missing something.

"I don't see them as rhythm games so much," said Matsuura of the games that followed *PaRappa*. "For example, to me, 'rhythm' was an important element of game design, so I embodied this by incorporating drum players' techniques, such as using both hands, or using them in alternate ways." For Matsuura, getting players to feel the rhythm is everything. In theory, you can ace a *Guitar Hero* track with the sound turned off and no natural sense of rhythm. It's not about teaching the player to develop their own internal metronome, but about memorizing button combinations. If a game doesn't require the player to demonstrate a sense of rhythm in the musical performance sense, he doesn't believe it should be labeled as such.

It's easy to misread or attribute incongruencies in older art and media to the passage of time and expectations, to assume that Matsuura and his team were trying to translate the reality of rapping through a cartoony mid-90s lens, and were simply held back by the limits of

12   Para Para is a type of synchronized dance that mainly utilizes upper-body movements; stylistically, it's similar to line dancing, and although it originated in Japan and was most popular in the 1980s through to the early 2000s, it's almost always used in conjunction with Eurobeat music.

technology. We incorrectly assume that fidelity was the goal and that creators we never met were simply doing their best.

Rapping is about rhythm, and *that* is what *PaRappa the Rapper* wants to communicate through its gameplay and scoring system. As we've established, all of the player-controlled actions are translated through six total inputs: the four face buttons on the PS1 controller, and the L1 and R1 shoulder buttons (simplified as a yellow "L" and a blue "R" in game). Every verse that PaRappa spits is communicated through those inputs, and while they're highly contextual, they're also predictable. Pressing the △ button four or five times in a row is how the player says "*Check and turn the signals to the...*" as well as "*Do I know why we stopped the car?*" in the same one-minute span in Stage 2, a driving level. Every button carries a lot of weight. Many players, myself included, will scramble to meet these prompts on time to avoid their score dipping low enough to require a do-over.

For instance, the inputs for "*Step* [△] *on the* [△] *gas* [O]" and "*Step* [△] *on the* [△] *brakes* [■]" are the same every time. But when you look down at the controller's face buttons, the three inputs are in an upwards-pointing triangle shape, essentially recreating the same physical motions your body makes to hit the gas (right) and brake (left) pedals while keeping your head (top) on the road. Each verse has its own inputs, and the inputs carry a logical consistency.

Later on, PaRappa is told to stop the car and recognize an imminent emergency: His driving instructor forgot to close the door. This verse "*You* [△] *forgot* [O] *to close* [×] *the door...* [■]" requires the player to hit all four face buttons in a clockwise sweep, as if they're scanning the entire car around them before proceeding. (The beat cuts out to pause on the door slamming, as Instructor Mooselini lets out a satisfied grunt of approval before the song kicks back to life. It's great.)

Nothing in *PaRappa's* gameplay is meant to mimic the act or mental process of rapping, but the button inputs all help the player become immersed in the context of each rhyme, and in the greater rhythm of each song's flow. It's not a rap simulator, it's a drumming-a-beat-on-a-cafeteria-table-during-lunch simulator.[13] Success or failure is a matter of following the programmed flow and rhythm, but high-level play can only be achieved by going beyond the written instructions.

"Rhythm comes naturally, in a way, from two or more vertical or horizontal behavioral components," Matsuura told me via email, referring to rhythm's succession of strong (or stressed) and weak hits. How those hits are combined is how a rhythm is formed so that in

---

13   "Grindin'" by Clipse is to tables and desks as "Toccata and Fugue in D minor" is to pipe organs.

a traditional rock song, the strong hit is on the down-beat and the weak hit is on the upbeat, while in genres like ska and reggae, that pattern is reversed. "There is a concept in drum play called *paradiddle*. Paradiddle consists of two single strokes by hand followed by a double stroke. An example would be to play symmetrical beats, like LRLLR or RLRRL. Paradiddle has a sublanguage element to it. I sometimes see [an] unexpected [relationship] between the [...] lyrics and rhythm [in this way]."

For the uninitiated, famous examples of paradiddle in drumming can be heard in the opening hi-hat rhythms of tracks like "Theme From Shaft" by Isaac Hayes and "Smoke on the Water" by Deep Purple. When you start to hear and feel each of *PaRappa*'s levels as something akin to a drum beat, with each button press like the rhythmic hit of a sampler pad (which is basically what's happening on a technical level), it entirely transforms how you play the game.

"I did not see many rhythm games released after *[PaRappa]*, which paid attention to this type of rhythm pattern," Matsuura says. "Stage 2 was made with this in mind, to strongly encourage users to use both hands."

I went back and played the entire game with both hands on the face buttons, the controller flat in front of me. It was weird, and different, and made a lot of the rhythmic patterns feel more natural. (To experience the difference, try drumming a rhythm with one hand, and then try drumming the same beat split across both hands.) Matsuura said that other games he had encountered before making *PaRappa* included plastic peripherals, but he dismissed them as focusing on "competition timing," instead of "rhythm gameplay." That's as true today as it was 30 years ago, because there's a huge difference between teaching someone to react to timing cues, and imbuing them with a natural sense of rhythm.

PaRappa the Rapper is a game about rapping that tries to give every player an inherent lesson about *rhythm*. Its scoring system is borderline inscrutable, to say nothing of COOL mode and its many secrets. It's a drum machine disguised as a children's toy, and rewards players who approach it from both sides of that spectrum.

But that core focus on rhythm came at a cost, and is why later ports of the game are even harder for players to enjoy, much less master, on a mechanical level. But for now, we know *how* to rap in *PaRappa*. Let's talk about *why* you do it.

IT'S ALL IN THE MIND

I FIND IT EASIEST TO ACCEPT *PaRappa* at face value. This is a game that opens with a combined three and a half minutes of cutscenes before any gameplay begins. The opening cutscene introduces the player to the main cast: PaRappa, PJ Berri, Katy Kat, and Sunny Funny. They finish watching a movie, head to a local restaurant, and give us insight into their personalities and motivations. Katy is vibrant and confident; sweet Sunny is the object of PaRappa's affections; PJ Berri is lazy and my personal hero; PaRappa is insecure and broke. As his friends order meals, PaRappa slouches up to the cash register and asks for the only thing he can afford: A glass of water.

And then the title screen drops.

After you start the game properly and begin Stage 1, you're treated to… more cutscenes. The scene at the restaurant continues, with two unnamed bullies (called "the Bad Guys" in the end credits) bursting through the front doors to immediately start hitting on Katy and Sunny. PaRappa seems ready to speak up when Sunny tells the Bad Guys to stop it. And then Joe Chin arrives. He's a "hero" right out of a comic book, bursting into the scene with his own fanfare and superhero pose to rush to the defense of Sunny and Katy.

Joe is the walking avatar of PaRappa's insecurity; he's rich, handsome, and confident. He's everything PaRappa believes he should be, and his presence often kicks off PaRappa's own quest for self-improvement in each level. After watching Joe de-escalate the situation, PaRappa imagines himself as a badass destroyer of men. He wants to get tougher. And for that he finds his first teacher.

If there's any character that threatens to eclipse PaRappa's popularity in his own games, it's Chop Chop Master Onion. He's the sole character the player interacts with in the demo of the first game, and he's the *only* character to have a dedicated song/level in each game of the *PaRappa/Um Jammer* trilogy, where he goes through an entire rags-to-riches arc. It's endearing and goofy and, I cannot stress this enough, involves a talking onion-man with visible stink lines emanating from his body.

There's a lot to love about the character and his first level, from the wholesome punny charm of his name (Rodney Greenblat named every character he designed), to the Wu-Tang-Clan-by-way-of-the-Commodores intensity of the level's beat. But some song lyrics sign up for permanent residence in the corner of your brain.

Kick! Punch! It's all in the mind
If you wanna test me, I'm sure you'll find
The things I'll teach ya is sure to beat ya
Nevertheless you'll get a lesson from teacher now

It's not "Juicy," or "Triumph," or even "Rapper's Delight." But in four lines (honestly, even just the very first one), this track tells the player everything they need to know. They'll be kicking and punching, they'll be learning from a teacher, but the lessons will have the cadence of a fight. Most crucially, they'll learn that it's "all in the mind."

Those are the type of verses that beg you to finish the phrase when you catch a snippet of them through a passing car's window, like Roger Rabbit bursting through a wall to finish the "shave and a haircut" musical gag. Call-and-response songs compel you to finish your side of the exchange, and *PaRappa the Rapper* is a collection of playable call-and-response songs at its core.

One person made it all possible: Ryu Watabe, the scarily multitalented Japanese rapper and musician who voices Chop Chop Master Onion (as well as Joe Chin) and provided the demo raps for every other character in the game, including PaRappa himself. Watabe brought the game's rapping to life, serving as the bilingual bridge between Masaya Matsuura's English-language music and composition and Gabin Itou's Japanese storyboarding and scenario writing.

Watabe was born in Tokyo, but his family moved to America before he was old enough to attend kindergarten. After high school (and following some guidance from his father), he moved back to Japan to learn more about where he came from. His bilingualism, dual passions for athletics and music, and post-secondary education in business gave him plenty of career options in Japan, where he worked as everything from a CNN interpreter to a suit-and-tie office worker. Eventually, he transitioned out of full-time work to spend more time working on his music career.

Through a musician friend, Watabe learned that Matsuura was looking for help with a rap-based video game. And that's how Itou, Matsuura, and Watabe wound up together in a studio, piecing together the entire game of *PaRappa the Rapper* in a creative environment that was part freestyle rap cypher and part animation storyboarding meeting. Matsuura and Itou explained the scenario for each level and the story leading up to it, and Watabe would start freestyling (in English) over Matsuura's track, based on his understanding of the scenario. The two of them went back and forth, tweaking beats and lyrics in separate recordings, until one song/level was done. Rinse, repeat, and six songs later, *PaRappa* was complete.

•

The only creative process that matters is the one that works for you, but that doesn't stop so many people (myself included) from poring over the process of artists they respect and admire, looking for the replicable piece of data that they can bring back into their own work. But the story Watabe shared—taken from an interview in the Japan-exclusive *PaRappa the Rapper Official Guide Book*—is liberating in how many rules the game's creators broke. There was no true father to the style of *PaRappa the Rapper*, no clear single point of inspiration. You don't need to be a genius to trace all the sources of inspiration that wound up in the final product—but it does help.

RapGenius.com was basically the homepage for my early twenties. Now known as simply "Genius," for its inclusion of all genres of music, Rap Genius was part song lyrics database and part hip hop book club. For the Napster generation of music fans/cyber criminals, Rap Genius provided all the liner notes we had been missing for years. Not only were your favorite rap lyrics archived and peer-reviewed for accuracy, they could be annotated and debated, line-by-line. I remember following fascinating debates in the depths of single lines of Wu-Tang songs, as people I'd never met argued if a verse was a direct *wuxia* film reference, or another brick in the great wall of the Clan's expansive slang dictionary.

Genius is still around, and still popular. But I'll always feel like its founders buckled and sold out when they removed the "Rap" from the name. What other musical genre could inspire that level of lyrical scrutiny?[14] In 2022, the top three most-viewed lyrics of all time on the site were all hip hop songs. "Despacito" is in the top spot, which is both a win for hip hop *and* bilingualism.

Any song can have its lyrics added to the site's archive, but a song riddled with user-added annotations commands another level of respect. I giggled with nerdy joy when I learned that artists as big as Lin-Manuel Miranda and Eminem[15] regularly create annotations for their own songs to clear up debates and add behind-the-scenes trivia.

And yes, the entire *PaRappa the Rapper* soundtrack is on Genius, fully annotated. It's a modest effort, with its most-popular song clocking in at just shy of twenty thousand views compared to the *23 million* of "Despacito (Remix)." But it shows a love and respect that speaks to the power of those verses, of these artists, of that opening line, a call-and-response that has stretched across decades.

14   Taylor Swift fans have entered the chat.
15   "Rap God" is the 2nd-most viewed song on Genius as of this writing.

Watabe's verses don't have pages of intense debate and analysis over their layers of meaning—they were never supposed to. Genius, like every other database fuelled mostly by passion and community, is where we store and commemorate songs we want to remember and those we couldn't forget if we tried.

JUST SITTIN'
IN THE CAR

ALMOST EVERY VIDEO game involves growth. Sometimes what improves is only the player's own skill: Play enough *Tetris*, you'll get better at *Tetris* thanks to your own internal growth. Other games portray your growth through game mechanics external to your own skill: leveling up in a Final Fantasy game, or gaining more powerful items in a Metroid game. Internal growth requires commitment, which can lead to quitting before you master that game's particular learning curve. But external growth is often just the *illusion* of improvement; if you hit level 99 in *Final Fantasy VII*, it doesn't mean you're a hundred times better at playing the game than you were at the start; you still mostly navigate menus and read text to proceed.

In real life, growth looks something like a mix of these two experiences. Skills require repetition and practice, and we're often clued into our growth when we notice objective changes in ourselves or the world around us. That feedback is crucial to gauging whether we're growing at all. But what's missing is the third, most organic part of becoming a better person: We all need someone to show us how to do it.

PaRappa the Rapper is a game about becoming a better version of yourself. From the opening cutscene to the final musical number, we are put in the red-and-white sneakers of a main character consumed by his perceived inadequacies. Lovelorn PaRappa is broke and constantly questioning his own worth because of it. PaRappa resolves to change his life and acquire all the things he's missing; he wants to be a "real man," but he can't do it alone. So he finds teachers.

In most games, we are challenged to "beat" a game or a boss—every new piece of software is essentially a duel to the death. PaRappa shifts the usual adversarial relationship between player and game to one of collaboration and growth. You don't *fight* your teachers,[16] you learn from them. And in *PaRappa the Rapper*, every level is a lesson—literally.

There is no universal language to video games. While similar skills may transfer between titles (I can

16 Even if they deserve it, like when my 5th Grade teacher—Mrs. Parebzak—confiscated my Tamagotchi during recess, held it until the end of the school year (several months later) and when I asked for its return on the last day of class, told me she had "given it to her daughter as a gift." I will never forget this. And now, neither will you.

pick up almost any platformer and get the hang of it immediately because of a *Mario*-heavy childhood) and many oddly specific quirks can be added to a gamer's vocabulary over time (money inside of breakable barrels, fully-cooked food lying on the ground), every game still has its own fresh syllabus to teach you.

But learning in a video game doesn't apply those skills back to real life. I can learn how to make Mario jump, but I can't study my own gameplay recordings of *Super Mario Odyssey* and suddenly do a triple somersault. (If that were the case, I'd have record-setting performances at the NBA Slam Dunk Contest far more often.)

In real life, meaningful growth needs to be paired with guidance from someone who knows what they're doing. It involves trial and error and usually results in tiny, personal victories: moments when you know you've grown, but the world doesn't stop to throw you a parade.

It looks like learning to drive.

•

PaRappa the Rapper doesn't directly sample any existing music. But there are clear musical references all over the soundtrack. I was a teenager when a friend of mine sent an MP3[17] they had downloaded from Kazaa[18] to me over MSN Messenger[19] with an all-caps descriptor: IT'S FROM PARAPPA. The attached file was "Turtles Have Short Legs" by experimental German rock band, CAN.

On first listen, the similarities are so striking, it's almost blatant. That opening, toy-like piano riff that leads into a plodding, playful combo of drums and bass. It *sounds* like how a turtle's footsteps should feel. Listening to both tracks, it seems almost impossible that Masaya Matsuura wouldn't have been acutely aware of "Turtles."

Recorded during the sessions that led to the band's seminal 1971 album *Tamo Yago*, "Turtles" was an under-the-radar single that was only released on 7" vinyl, and generally fell between the cracks in the band's greater discography. But their lead singer during this era, Damo Suzuki, was a Japanese musician and a blazing figure in both the wider prog rock scene and the German genre

---

17   In the pre-streaming internet era, most MP3s were Linkin Park songs.

18   An online file-sharing program that was exactly like Napster, Limewire, or Morpheus, yet we all got weirdly tribalistic about our theft-platforms of choice.

19   A type of text messaging program/song lyric sharing service you could only access via computer. Ground zero for at least a dozen of my personal milestones and tragedies as a teenager.

of *krautrock*, a term that I will honestly try to use every chance I get.

It's almost certain that this old prog rock track served as the inspiration for "Instructor Mooselini's Rap." And none of it really matters.

Hip hop is an art form built on creative reappropriation. So it's all too fitting that one of the standout tracks from *PaRappa*'s soundtrack encapsulates all of this in its own beat. But writing it off as a simple interpolation of an existing song ignores all the unique, playful directions the track takes, especially in its entirely original beats for when the player is Rappin' BAD or AWFUL. Instead, the track's nod to CAN only enhances *PaRappa the Rapper*'s adherence to basically every core pillar of old school hip hop.

But most importantly, the beat fucking *slaps*. Sometimes, that's all you really need to stay timeless.

•

Stage 2 of *PaRappa the Rapper* opens with the customary minutes-long cutscene setting up PaRappa's newest dilemma: Joe Chin is back.

There is no final boss or chief antagonist in *PaRappa*; it's a *Mario* game where Bowser is your own self-doubt, and Princess Peach is your sense of self-respect. But Joe Chin unlocks all of PaRappa's insecurities with his mere presence. When I first played the game, I saw Chin as a blowhard and a bully—the classic rom-com rival who PaRappa needed to show up to win Sunny's heart.

Playing it now, I see a situation that's far truer to my own problems and insecurities. Joe Chin is just doing his own thing, yet PaRappa cannot help but see everything in the world around him as a jab at his own shortcomings. None of PaRappa's friends tell him he's not manly enough; he invents that narrative inside his own head. And at the start of Stage 2, the gang wants to hit the beach, but none of them have their driver's license. Cue: Joe Chin, driving some sort of a combination between a stretch limo and the hot mess of a car ("The Homer") that Homer designs on *The Simpsons*.[20]

PJ and PaRappa end up sitting in the back of the limo, and somehow end up drenched in jacuzzi water and covered in donuts. Once again, PaRappa has a daydream where he imagines what life would be like if he could drive, with him and Sunny, in a *Grease*-like flying convertible, having the time of their lives. His mission becomes clear: He needs that driver's license, so he comes under the tutelage of Instructor Mooselini, the driving teacher.

---

20   This scene also features one of my favorite line reads in the entire game, where PJ Berri starts to gush over the car's top speed, but just trails off into a meaningless garble of made up numbers. Joy is always the goal.

In its best moments, *PaRappa the Rapper* lets players experience moments they've lived or felt themselves, but with a candy coating of cartoon whimsy and musicality added for some extra flavor. It all comes together to create a perfect distillation of not just the experience of being a nervous teen on your first road test, but how the *world around you* can feel, when you're one government document away from freedom.

This sense of barely-contained excitement kept in check by the rigid standards of a driving test can be found in every aspect of this stage. First and foremost is the Queen Latifah-adjacent vocal performance laid down by veteran singer Saundra Williams (credited as "Sandra" during the original game's end credits) as Mooselini. Williams takes simple everyday phrases ("I forgot to close the door") and makes them her own the way only the best performers can.[21] As familiar as her voice had become after decades of hearing those lyrics in my head, it was no substitute for the moment she picked up the phone to tell me about her one-day marathon recording session for *PaRappa*.

•

For Saundra Williams, working on *PaRappa the Rapper* was just another gig. By the time she was approached

---

21   Further examples: How RZA from the Wu-Tang Clan pronounces "Swords," how Lauryn Hill pronounces "Thing," or how MF DOOM pronounced literally any string of words.

for the role by a producer friend in 1996, her career was already full of highlights—like winning talent night at the legendary Apollo Theater *four separate times*. By that point, she was in her early 30s and had a teenage son at home. Then—like now—her life consisted of finding singing gigs, being part of studio recordings, and going on tour. Across all the interviews and testimonials I could find with the PaRappa voice cast, one thing remains consistent: a recording session for a strange little video game role is just another gig for a working musician. History doesn't feel like history when it happens—it feels like work.

Williams's session for *PaRappa* was relatively straightforward—she was paid somewhere in the area of $250 to $350 by her producer intermediary, and was told to visit his Brooklyn brownstone recording studio to meet the client.

"There were two Japanese men [in the studio]," she recalls.[22] "They were very particular, they were really nice. But they were specific. And they told me what my character was: a stern driving instructor. Instructor Mooselini!"

For the next six or seven hours, well into the evening, Williams laid out all of her character's audio in a

---

22   One of these men was almost certainly Masaya Matsuura, who led the recording sessions. The other man, though less certain, may have been Gabin Itou, the game's story/scenario writer.

single session. She had no full script of the game to read from or detailed character concepts to look at. The process was relatively freeform, with Matsuura telling her the scenario as she went along. She stood at a mic stand with lyric sheets in front of her, hearing the demo track for the beat and Ryu Watabe's demo vocals for Mooselini and PaRappa running through her headphones.

"When I was in that studio room with these guys, I remember those lights being dim. I wanted to have that energy as if I were in a car," she says. "I remember the four of us being there, and just creating Instructor Mooselini's personality and energy in that room."

She recalls being asked for a lot of repeated takes, delivering the same handful of lines with different timing, emphasis, and energy. ("Do you know why we stopped the car again?" was an especially tricky line read.) It took hours of work to record a track that would ultimately clock in at under four minutes.

"I was hitting it again and again and again," she says. "But I had to have such a big, gregarious personality [to portray Mooselini]. I really enjoyed that session." Williams couldn't recall the exact material they covered beyond her character's feature song, but because that one session comprised her only interaction with Matsuura, NanaOn-Sha, or Sony as a whole, we can assume that all her audio (a handful of cutscene lines, her vocals on the ballad "Funny Love," and her verse in Stage 5) were also recorded then.

Williams headed home, and it was over. She didn't hear anything until months later, after the game's Japanese release. Which is where this story starts to sound upsettingly familiar to anyone who has followed the history of talented Black musicians.

Williams made it very clear that sharing her experience with me was not about malice or revenge; she just wanted to tell the whole story. A few months after *PaRappa the Rapper*'s Japanese release, she received a call at her mother's house from a woman who said she was from Sony.

"The woman was so nice," Williams recalls. "She said 'I wanted to tell you that *PaRappa the Rapper*, the video game you worked on? It has blown through the roof!' And they wanted to give me $7,000 or $5,000 on top of the $4,000 they had already paid me." Williams was confused: $4,000?

It turns out that the producer intermediary (unknowingly to everyone else) pocketed the majority of the agreed-upon rate for Williams, and threw her a few hundred dollars for hours of demanding work and expertise.

"I was just devastated," she says. "Because I'm the type of person who's like: 'Yo, you can do whatever you want, say whatever you want. But don't mess with my money, because that's how I eat.' It felt like people were making money all around my head, and I didn't." The woman from Sony Music took the complaint seriously, and the bonus was paid directly to Williams. But her original amount was gone.

"Young kids out here might be making these same decisions, and you really got to be smart about the moves you make," Williams says in retrospect. "But you never expect it to be someone you know. Because if that woman had not called? I never would have known."

Talking to Saundra Williams, I realized I had never talked to a Black woman who was involved in creating a major video game before. Every time I've watched a behind-the-scenes video or interviewed a developer, I was facing those same dimly-lit rooms full of White guys I imagined as a kid.

What Williams takes away from *PaRappa* isn't that she got burnt; it's everything that came afterwards: the physical copy she was gifted by Sony that she still has to this day, the experience of watching her son playing it with his friends and hearing his mom's voice, and of going to the GameStop a friend of hers operated and being treated "like a celebrity."

Williams continues to find new fans and is sent clips of her song being remixed on TikTok or turned into memes on YouTube. Her work in that brownstone studio endures and transforms in formats that are more accessible than the original game is today. That also means that her performance as Mooselini has re-emerged at a very different moment in pop culture analysis and awareness than when it debuted.

I've struggled with what to make of Instructor Mooselini.[23] She sounds like a Black woman, and is portrayed as a large, irritable, dark brown-skinned moose. Her nostrils flare and shoot out steam at points, and she spends most of her onscreen time frowning or scowling. But she's also kind, supportive, funny, and an accurate portrayal of how a driving instructor *feels* to interact with during your first road test. Yet Mooselini does not exist in a cultural vacuum.

The history of how anthropomorphized characters voiced by Black people can end up embodying racial stereotypes is long and messy, from the subservient and caricatured Faun, named Sunflower, in Disney's *Fantasia* (1940) to the choice to have the only Black woman in the English dub of *Aggretsuko*'s (2018) first season portray a gorilla named Gori. Williams tells me that many of her friends in the present take a dimmer view of Mooselini today.

"They say that it's obviously a Black lady's voice, and the character is brown, and a moose, and she's not the most attractive thing in the world. She's cute to me, but you know," she adds with a laugh. "And they just

23   Or her sister in the sequel, Instructor Moosesha.

feel like it's a bad caricature for the voice to be Black. And I don't really agree; I didn't really feel anything until they said that."

"Being a brown-skinned African American woman, I'm proud of that. I look in the mirror and I see beauty, but when I walk away from the mirror and out into society, I get the microaggressions all through the day— in professional settings, all over the world, because of how I look, or my hair. So I understand the sensitivity, but it doesn't have to apply to everything," Williams says.

"And maybe I'm blind to it, but I just don't want to think of it that way. But I can see it, and understand what my friends are saying," she says, before concluding, "If a moose in a game is really vexing your spirit, then you need to broaden your horizons and pick up a flagpole for something else."

One of my earliest childhood books was *Brer Rabbit and the Tar Baby*, using the character designs and framing from Disney's *Song of the South*. When I eventually learned that one of the books that taught me to love reading is historically, famously, erased-from-the-Disney-vaults levels of racist, I didn't feel great. But the worst part was finding scans of that old book as an adult, and feeling my stomach sink down to my shoes. The immediate power of racist imagery is to make its subject feel othered and less-than—the butt of the joke.

It makes you want to find the person who did it and ask them, point-blank, "Is this all I am to you?" (But you don't. Because you know the answer.)

I look at Instructor Mooselini, and I don't see a joke, or a caricature, or a window into the closely-held prejudices of her creators. If someone else sees that, I won't argue with them; representation is personal like that. But there are so many overt, cruel, pointed examples of racist caricatures there even today. I want to celebrate this as a win, so I will. I know what it feels like to be made into the joke, and after learning about what Saundra Williams did to bring Mooselini to life, it only feels like more of a triumph.

•

Between the earworm beat and the authenticity of Saundra Williams's vocals, we know that "Instructor Mooselini's Rap" is great. But it's paired with an almost Richard Scarry-esque portrayal of driving through a city. The world around PaRappa and Mooselini is an unbroken corridor of buildings with no room in between them, where street signs pop into your peripheral vision as the pair swerves and screeches around otherwise empty streets. The world folds into nothingness behind them, as if their car is driving along the surface of an endlessly-turning cylinder. As soon as the level starts, the hood of your car comes loose and flies away, giving the player a good look at the dual sets of color-coded pedals inside.

The Old-Timey Piano Music[24] that forms the melodic hook of the rap evokes the slapstick feel of a Buster Keaton film. It's a really novel attempt at conveying "teenagers learning to drive" through visuals, audio, and gameplay.

When I was seventeen years old, I was in the same place. Out of some misguided attempt to cram all my teenage milestones into the last few months of an extremely nerdy and unsexy high school experience, I found myself in a car with a stern Jamaican instructor named Greg, taking my first-ever road test on a weekday morning I took off from school. My plan(?) was to get my license, borrow a car(??), and drive my date to prom a few weeks later so we could go to the Canadian suburb equivalent of Makeout Point(???) afterwards.

I sat down beside Greg, buckled up, and—*no word of a lie*—said the phrase, "Alright, we're here, just sittin' in the car," to myself under my breath. As I pulled out of the lot, I could hear the piano riff from this level blasting from my mental boom box. I was ready.

I turned the steering wheel the wrong way during a parallel park and politely nudged my training vehicle into the driver's side door of the parked car beside me. I then apologized to Greg, turned the wheel the wrong

---

24   The official genre name.

way *again*, and nudged it a bit less politely. He offered/ threatened to drive me back to the driving center, but I turned him down and used my thousand-yard stare to keep an eye on traffic during the deathly silent trip back.

I still don't know how to drive. Sometimes life isn't an upward trend of milestones conquered and boxes checked; it's an often embarrassing mix of technical wins and humiliating losses. Few games give you any wiggle room between "heroic victory" and "literal death," but *PaRappa* does. Half the fun of playing the Car Level is losing, as the smooth main melody gives way to frantic train robbery music and violent cross-lane swerving. *PaRappa* does more to showcase the breadth of everyday life in a half dozen 3-minute chunks than other games do in their entire 60-hour runtimes.

Cars are a cultural shorthand for freedom, especially in North America. But even for pedestrian teens who spend their prom night dateless with friends in a Denny's parking lot, the next big milestone *PaRappa* tackles is far more universal: Being broke as hell.

MONEY, MONEY, MONEY—IT'S ALL YOU NEED

THE SETUP FOR STAGE 3 (Chapter: "My Dad's Gonna Bite Me!") and its song ("Prince Fleaswallow's Rap") follows a classic teen sitcom plot after PaRappa earns his driver's license. Within ten minutes, he's taking his dad's beater of a car out on the road to pick up his crew for an afternoon joyride. Sunny rides shotgun, with Katy Kat and PJ Berri in the backseat, and the car moves through the world with the grace and gravity of a Hot Wheels toy in the hands of a toddler. It does a backflip off a cliff and lands on the road without a hitch, and Sunny mentions that she wishes they could drive "someplace private."

Most of *PaRappa*'s levels kick off as a result of our hero's daydreaming, and that's what happens here. Taking Sunny's innocuous(?) comment as a hint towards a grand romantic gesture, PaRappa imagines them sipping sparkling apple juice on an oceanview terrace at sunset. Just as he imagines going in for their first kiss, his car drifts into oncoming traffic, and they crash into an eighteen-wheeler. The impact sends the car literally flying into Earth's orbit (Katy leans out the window to take pictures) before it crashes down where it launched, collapsing into a scrap heap in the middle of the street. Everyone is uninjured, because cartoon logic reigns supreme.

PaRappa's hard-won independence has adorably blown up in his face.

Part of childhood is being shielded from wider consequences, but adulthood means realizing their full scope. The day you get your driver's license can feel like the start of a countdown to your first auto-related incident. Mostly they manifest as fender benders or hitting local wildlife, but the immediate realness of *causing a problem that affects the outside world* is shocking.

In other words, it can feel like getting knocked into outer space. PaRappa imagines his father (delightfully portrayed as a put-upon, jowly dog in a tiny fedora and high-waisted pants) expressing his unchecked disappointment at the car accident: He still had "59 monthly installments to pay."[25] PaRappa's fuckup means he needs cash, so he takes a job trying to sell items at a flea market,

---

25 There are two types of people: Those who have to measure time in terms of bill payments, and those who don't.

and meets his third teacher, the reggae bullfrog Master Prince Fleaswallow (voiced by the late Lenky Don).

It's a tonal departure from the other levels in the game, and I'd bet that it's the least popular of all six playable songs. But intentionally or not, it made me feel seen.

Do well-off White kids go to flea markets? If they did, I don't remember seeing them. An immediate survey of White people I know resulted in the following responses: "Do you mean 'garage sales?'"; "Kind of."; "Not until I was in college." But it's another one of those easy-to-ignore tone and setting choices in *PaRappa the Rapper* that hit different if you come at them with the right context.

•

An ex of mine once showed me something I thought only existed in fiction: an ornate crest of heraldry, fashioned out of aged wood. She said it was her family's symbol, and they could chase their lineage back across centuries in a clear, flowing family tree like the ones I tried but could never manage to complete for elementary school assignments. My family's background spans through Indian diaspora and African American slavery, so colonialism makes it almost impossible to track anything further than a few generations. If you've ever had to move in a hurry, you know that something will always be left behind, like your favorite necklace, or all physical records of your family's lineage.

It's been hard to get a straight story from my mom and grandma about what they went through to give me enough of a privileged foundation that I can cross "PlayStation historian" off my bucket list. My mom has emphasized multiple times that we were never truly *broke*, and that even when income was shaky and we may have been lightly couch-surfing, my brother and I were never hungry or harmed.

But I think of myself back at 28 (drunk, traveling the world, trying to find a charger for his Nintendo 3DS) and I compare it to her at 28 (sober, somehow), keeping two kids alive. I imagine my grandma, who was born in Kolkata in the middle of World War II and completely unaware that her father was serving as a combat medic, choosing (decades later) to give up her hard-won condo to once again dip into active parenthood. The gulf between the constant sacrifice of minority immigrant parents and the comparatively privileged lives they offer their children creates a specific kind of guilt shared by second-gen immigrant children.

My mom won't ever tell me how bad things were for her, because she doesn't want me to feel liable for her sacrifices. I'm also convinced that if first-generation immigrants ever allowed themselves to fully process the trauma they went through to survive, they'd all collectively snap, like a bunch of *Rambos: First Blood*.[26] We weren't *poor*, but the difference between my family and my friends' families became most pronounced when swapping stories about the non-essentials: their vacations and cottages and camps vs. our libraries and community centers and boredom. The friends that never had to balance after-school clubs with work shifts, and didn't take a year off after graduation to save for university tuition. Through these conversations, you learn the limits of your life.

Parenting kids with ADHD is all about recognizing and working within the limits of what your chaotic children will allow. So if you need to take the family to Costco, the errand needs to be turned into a game, a distraction, or both. If my brother and I had understood how those trips were just our parents doing mundane things like "buying supplies so we don't die," we would have rioted from the sheer boredom of it all. But in my mind, they were the social events of the month.

Costco (capitalism's passive-aggressive answer to the question "How much is too much?") made it acceptable for my brother and me to run around, get lost, and find our way back to Mom's shopping cart. We were given missions that savvy readers will recognize as "Child Labor Fetch Quests," but they gave us a sense of purpose: Who could find the family-sized pack of

---

26   Rejected alternate joke: *Mom-bo: First Bloodline.*

paper towels first? We arrived around late morning, filling ourselves up with food samples and scoring seconds through a mix of racially ambiguous charm and rigorously enforced politeness. Only years later did I realize this was a way to score a free lunch for the whole family while also getting some errands done.

Flea markets entered the scene in my teens, especially when I started working. Mom has always had an eye for deals; when I tell her I've paid full price for something, I watch in real time as her pride in me fades from her face. She has furnished entire homes through Facebook Marketplace and Kijiji.[27] My favorite one was the 747 Flea Market in Brampton, named for its proximity to the Toronto Pearson Airport. I spent hours there, haggling, buying pirated media, and scanning for whatever deal I'd use to justify the entire trip. Well into my 20s, my brother and I would climb into Mom's car—unlike me, he pushed through a couple of failed driving tests until he succeeded—and find a new flea market to lazily speculate for a few hours.

Those weekends spent chasing free samples and flea market deals gave me a world where people looked and acted like me and the people I loved. The 747 Flea Market let me buy Polish pierogies and Trinidadian

---

27 A popular Canadian alternative to Craigslist, Kijiji was developed by eBay employees from Quebec in the mid-2000s and is now branded as eBay Classifieds worldwide.

doubles on the same lunchtray before I bought a burnt CD full of Jamaican dancehall riddims and let an Indian Aunty pressure me into some horrible fashion choices. I now recognize that I grew up in an abnormally diverse pocket of North American culture, which made its absence in the media I loved even more disappointing.

In the mid-2000s, I could count on one hand the amount of times I had seen Black or Indian characters positively portrayed in media. I had seen plenty of things that I *thought* were okay at the time, and only understood their distortion later.[28] It was so much stereotype, and so little substance.

•

Despite mostly showing up in sports, racing, and crime games, hip hop now has a regular presence in video game soundtracks today. But reggae and dancehall music are essentially nonexistent. There's a very good chance that *PaRappa the Rapper* features the first reggae song with lyrics in video game history.

Lenky Don's vocals are booming and relaxed in equal measures, walking the player through the rhyme-heavy, downtempo flow of the song. The level introduces rapid notes placed in quick succession and amps up use of the L1 and R1 buttons. The lyrics themselves

---

28   *Indiana Jones and the Temple of Doom* was one of my favorite movies as a child, and my Grandma hated it. I get it now.

are ridiculous and contradictory, with Fleaswallow saying that the key to selling "is love," but capping the level with the double refrain of "Money, money, money / It's all you need" while his eyes turn into literal dollar signs.

As the wise old frog gives PaRappa some on-the-job training, his verses are part confessional, part boastful: He claims to be "the number one ruler of the seven seas" before ultimately admitting that he has "never sold everything, everything." In the blink of an eye, his wares (a single bottle cap, a lucky stuffed skunk, a rug with his face on it) are sold for piles of gold coins to unseen customers. Background details suggest he also sells used hubcaps and reads palms on request. "Fleaswallow" is charmingly relaxed compared to the stages that both precede and follow it.

Masaya Matsuura's decision to include a reggae song in a game ostensibly about rapping shows a nuanced historical eye toward the hip hop genre. The musical and stylistic lineage of 90s rap and hip hop can be traced back to ska and reggae, but those roots weren't obvious if you were listening to top 40 rap hits at the time. A few years later, the post-millennium breakthroughs of Shaggy and Sean Paul made their shared DNA both abundantly clear and financially lucrative. And today, rappers seed their rhymes with accents and slang stolen wholesale from dancehall culture despite not coming from it themselves.[29]

But… real talk? It's *my* least favorite song and level in the game as well. It's not weird or catchy enough[30] to become a true earworm. But I'm glad it's there, because it shows how much the team at NanaOn-Sha *wanted* this style of music to be represented. Just like those Saturday afternoons at the flea market, it gave me a brief glimpse of myself in a passing reflection.

---

29   Some of those unnamed, extremely popular rappers may even come from Toronto.

30   *Gitaroo Man*, a PS2-era cult classic rhythm game that follows in PaRappa's footsteps, has a vastly superior reggae/dub track of its own: "Nuff Respect."

EVERY SINGLE DAY, STRESS COMES IN EVERY WAY

The Chicken Level.

By many accounts, it's the hardest level in the game. As one YouTube commenter puts it, "I had kidney stones that were easier to pass than this level."

In all subsequent remakes, it's riddled with more input/timing errors than any other part of *PaRappa the Rapper*. It rolls out a style of rap that has never existed in our world—like Julia Child meets Young-Holt Unlimited. Getting a COOL ranking is the stuff of legend among dedicated players, and its core concept—baking a seafood cake—is wacky even for this game. It has also been playing in my brain, nonstop, for twenty years.

Stage 4 ("Guaranteed to Catch Her Heart"), starring Cheap Cheap The Cooking Chicken as its Rap Master, is everything great about *PaRappa the Rapper* as a playable animated musical. It will change how you approach even mundane physical actions like cracking eggs and mixing flour. It also offers you access to the most valuable teacher of all: Failure.

You will fail *so goddamn much.*

PaRappa the Rapper takes place over an unspecified amount of time, which works in the game's favor to really make you feel like each level is a self-contained ten-minute episode of a lost cartoon you didn't know you needed. PaRappa completes Stage 3 with enough cash not only to fix his Dad's car, but also to upgrade it into a smiling coupe with a mirror sheen. Stage 4 shifts focus to Katy Kat rallying PaRappa and PJ to help plan Sunny's birthday party. They play a game of *janken* (a Japanese variant of rock-paper-scissors that goes completely unexplained to international audiences), and PaRappa ends up on cake duty.

He heads over to the Sweety Cakes Fresh Bake Shop, which is helpfully shaped like a giant two-tiered cake. After checking out all the options (including the "Total Love" Cake, selling for $437.25), he settles on the simple "Daisy" cake ($22.95), which is, like all good birthday cakes, in the shape of the birthday girl's head. And then Mister Fucking Perfect himself, Joe Chin, shows up.

Chin wobbles into the frame carrying a wedding-style cake wider than his torso and taller than the screen, and starts rattling off the artistic intent behind every tier. The camera pans up into the stratosphere as his dialogue speeds up into a rapid chipmunk-esque blur, showing us all of the objects caught in its towering monument to baked goods: a mountain climber, a woodpecker, three construction signs drawn with crayon, an entire airplane, and a cell phone tower. The 42nd (and final) tier is topped with an effigy of Chin and Sunny, as he declares it the capstone to their future relationship.

It's *a lot*, in every sense of the phrase. Up until this point, all of PaRappa's anxieties have been mostly of his own invention. His insecurity now becomes our own, and when Joe Chin pats PaRappa on the back as a goodbye gesture, he's sent tumbling face-first into the Daisy Cake. Once again, PaRappa daydreams about the worst possible outcome: Katy screaming at him when he arrives at Sunny's party empty-handed.

Through the power of his iconic mantra "I gotta believe!", he once again finds a solution: He'll bake a damn cake himself. Which brings both PaRappa and the player to "Cheap Cheap the Cooking Chicken's Show." As the narrator says, the day's dish will be Seafood Cake, "guaranteed to catch her heart."

Within three minutes, you'll have lost, and the real lesson begins.

•

So many video games are about matters of life and death. A player character eliminating and being eliminated by enemies has been a mainstay of the artform since 1962's *Spacewar!* Mario dispatches enemies in cartoon puffs of clouds and sparkles, and is thrown off the bottom of the player's screen itself whenever the player loses.

My babysitter growing up had a television older than any I had ever seen. It was *huge*, with knobs to change channels and a built-in set of bunny-eared antennae, its tubes and wires encased in an even bigger wood-paneled chassis. The bottom of their TV, underneath the screen, was designed to look like a long pull-out drawer. It had burnished brass detailing and a handle. But it was just for show; it never opened, which only drove my imagination to new heights. After school, my brother and I gathered with her kids to watch one of three TV channels, or to take turns playing *Super Mario World*, round-robin style.

As four children under the age of ten playing Mario, we died a lot. And every time, Mario and Luigi threw their hands above their heads in despair and disappeared through the bottom of the screen, right down into that impossible drawer. I imagined finding the right key and finally opening the drawer, only to uncover the dead bodies of hundreds of pixelated plumbers. I wanted to set them free, or scatter their remains in the backyard.

Years later, I correctly identified this thought as "pretty fucking metal."

I was not an especially hardcore, angsty, or cool child, but playing *Super Mario World* made me acutely aware of the inherent objective of kill-or-be-killed baked into almost every game. We beat bosses, we lose lives. But we're also essentially immortal. With some very notable exceptions, death isn't permanent in games; it's a setback at best and an artificial start-over point at worst. Every player guides their avatar through their own personal *samsara*, dying and being reborn until they reach the enlightenment of the end credits.

If you're a longtime fan of video games and introduce them to a relative newcomer, the cognitive dissonance can be fascinating. Much like growing up in a strict household or having low self-esteem (or both), watching someone unfamiliar with games struggle with rules and norms you accepted years ago makes you question why you ever accepted that standard of treatment to begin with. When my wife asks why Mario games have lives, it's easy to say that it's simply a holdover from gaming's arcade roots. But that's not really an explanation for why it still exists.

Gaming is the rare artform that often requires technical proficiency to see through to the end, and as more games seek acclaim not for their gameplay prowess but for things like audio visuals and story, it only leads to more tension between the wide ocean of storytelling and the brick wall of gamer skill checks. If someone wants to experience the story of *The Last of Us*'s Ellie and Joel, they also have to be intimately familiar with 3D camera control, stealth game mechanics, crafting systems, and over-the-shoulder shoot-and-cover gameplay.

Basic game design logic dictates that if you can kill enemies, they should be able to kill you back. And if you can't kill enemies, what does the player even do? This is a question still being wrestled with today, but *PaRappa* provided one of many compelling alternatives in 1997. It's a game full of action and conflict and zero violence. It's a game without health bars that still clearly (and dramatically) conveys the player's pending success or failure.

Failure in *PaRappa* doesn't mean death or anything worse than failing your driving test or, later, shitting your pants in public.[31] It often results in embarrassment or a reprimand, just as failure does in real life. We fail in tons of ways that aren't threats to our mortality, yet we still feel emotionally *shook* when failure happens. *PaRappa's* consequences are minor, but they can feel like the world is ending. What's more teenage than that?

PaRappa isn't a rapper by trade. He's a teenager doing his best. So in turn this isn't a game about "becoming a rapper," it's a game about *being a kid that likes to*

---

31   See you in four chapters!

rap. I won't say that the events in the game aren't happening literally—that's a disservice to its intentionally playful cartoon logic—but it's more that we're watching PaRappa connect with his teachers and internalize their lessons through rap. All but one level are instructional, conversational hip hop tracks where both PaRappa and his Rap Master narrate their thoughts and actions over a beat. It's a town where the mother tongue is hip hop, and everyone is fluent.

The ironic part of rhythm games—*PaRappa* included—is that despite their often stimulating visual presentation, the player's eyes stay glued to wherever the relevant visual prompts are presented. In *PaRappa*, I rarely take my eyes off the button cues at the top of the screen, while in *Guitar Hero* and *Rock Band*, I'm watching the circular nodes at the bottom. Feedback on failure or bad performance usually comes through an interruption to the audio track (as in *Rock Band* and countless others), or an overwhelming mix of visual and audio cues engineered to make you feel bad.

PaRappa takes a different route. Unlike later games in the genre, the player doesn't hit buttons to make a song happen. PaRappa *is* your instrument, and he makes sounds whether or not your timing is correct. Cutting out his vocals can't serve as an audio cue for failure, so Matsuura and the NanaOn-Sha team did the next best thing: They created unique versions of songs for each ranking of every song in the game.

As you climb or fall in the ranks, the backing track shifts over in turn. Even better, each track version also comes with a custom set of visual changes to the level, with the worst and best ends of the spectrum becoming surreal scenes of artistic chaos.

The average player wants a GOOD rank; anything below that risks failure. So any time spent in BAD or AWFUL is to be avoided at all costs. The developers knew that whole backing tracks and visual experiences in each level would be actively avoided or, as we will later explore, inaccessible to the majority of players. And they did it anyway. They made failure a reward in and of itself—a way of seeing or experiencing something new.

They also made failure *so goddamn weird*.

•

Stage 4 begins with PaRappa watching Cheap Cheap's cooking show on TV. He's at his kitchen counter, following along with her rap/instructions. The scene cuts between hovering shots of PaRappa at work and the Cooking Chicken giving a lesson while framed by the bezel of a TV set as if PaRappa is watching the show. When you're Rappin' GOOD, the level functions as a simple back-and-forth, and Cheap Cheap's vocal performance is mixed to sound like it's coming from a slightly fuzzy radio broadcast. That performance, delivered by the late Michelle Burks (who also voices Katy Kat in *PaRappa* and *Lammy*), finds the perfect spot between Martha Stewart and Julia Child and becomes unforgettable in the process. The song's beat is a devastatingly catchy combo of a classic breakbeat, a funky guitar riff, an equally funky bassline, and the only saxophone sample in the entire game.

When you clear the stage, its ultimate visual gag is revealed: PaRappa and Cheap Cheap have been performing on the same "stage" the entire time, literally side by side. She flies over to him, gives him a congratulatory line, and you win the level. Like every other visual gag in the game, it's presented matter-of-factly, with no interest in analyzing the meta-ness of it all. You have a goddamn Seafood Cake to deliver.

If you're Rappin' BAD or AWFUL, the playful gag turns into a threat. When (yes, *when*) the player's ranking drops one level to BAD, Cheap Cheap walks stage-right from her counter to PaRappa's, getting all up in his face as the level's backing track transforms without skipping a beat.

There's something primal about games that give the player a warning alarm when they're in danger. Franchises like Zelda and Pokémon have featured a pervasive, rhythmic beeping when the player is almost out of health. I always took it to be a way of indicating a character's heartbeat, beating steadily until you either died or healed.[32] Pokémon's fifth generation of titles (*Black* and *White* and their direct numerical sequels) took this idea to its natural conclusion, turning the low-HP beeping into the foundation of an original song that only plays when the player is in critical danger during battles.

In the PaRappa games and *Um Jammer*, the "you're failing" sound is not anything as clear as a buzzer or a beep; it's like the laughter of an inflatable squeaky rubber duck, a pitch-shifted metronome of taunts. As soon as you drop into BAD status, the sound becomes a constant part of the beat. But every song has a different part of its beat emphasized or stripped away as your Rappin' goes from BAD to AWFUL.

Countless other music games will halt or cut the music as a punishment, but *PaRappa* strips it down, because even a lesson that's going catastrophically poorly has value, and you're always just a few tight bars away from redeeming the entire song. More crucially, the player is never robbed of the tools they need to carry a rhythm.

So when you hit BAD and Cheap Cheap decides to completely disregard PaRappa's personal space, angrily

---

32 Many modern shooters and survival horror games just include an actual heartbeat sound, turning a lo-fi flourish into a literal cue.

narrowing her eyes and flapping her wings as he tries to combine perch and clams into a baked dessert, her vocal track becomes crystal clear during the transition. But at the same time, the saxophone melody is lost. The drums and bassline are intact until you hit AWFUL.

At this point, Cheap Cheap's entire feathery face turns red as she literally hops with *rage* at your culinary incompetence, a poultry version of Gordon Ramsay. The bassline is cut, leaving only that guitar riff and the drum beat to guide you back to a GOOD ranking. If the player can't end the song on a GOOD ranking (or if they fall to an unnamed ranking lower than AWFUL), they reach the singular fail state of a level, where the Rap Master simply shuts the whole thing down and tells PaRappa (and the player) to try again.

These fail states range from disappointed teachers simply telling you to take it from the top (Chop Chop Master Onion, Instructor Mooselini), to public humiliation (Stages 5 and 6), to Cheap Cheap *rage-laying an egg* that instantly hatches an angry chick that tells you to do better.[33]

And in each level, a negative Rappin' status essentially grants the player a new version of the song. A BAD performance with Chop Chop Master Onion has the bouncy accordion riffs of the normal track cut out and replaced with a menacing bassline that sounds

---

33   Awesome.

straight out of an early Eminem or Mobb Deep album. Slip down to AWFUL, and the entire track is just drums and dramatic violin hits reminiscent of a martial arts movie (or a Wu-Tang Clan song), as Master Onion lies on his side, too disappointed to even stand up and demonstrate his moves.

Instructor Mooselini's piano riff even has an entirely different tune for both BAD and AWFUL modes, abandoning the (allegedly) CAN-inspired beat for an unbroken piano riff that evokes damsels being tied to railroad tracks in a silent film. Prince Fleaswallow's rap changes the least as your performance drops, but the song still sounds more stripped down as you fall from BAD to AWFUL. His flea market stall begins to sag and collapse around PaRappa, with an AWFUL performance leading to a giant golden sombrero unexpectedly falling on his head, blocking PaRappa's vision until his rapping improves.

In the world of *PaRappa*, your actions have immediate consequences in how each stage looks and sounds. But the player is never robbed of the basic rhythm and lyrics they'd need to fix their own mess and keep playing. Things get weird and messy, but you've got a shot. You'll still fail a *lot*, but it doesn't feel like punishment.

Of course, tough love kindness is a very fine line. The Chicken Level is only a fair test if the game itself is playing fair; to perform a task perfectly requires perfect tools. And the first major crack in our ability to enjoy the game today is exposed by this stage.

PaRappa the Rapper has a port problem, and the industry as a whole has a music games problem.

REMIXED &
REMASTERED

In 2017, Sony celebrated the twentieth anniversary of *PaRappa the Rapper* with some cute retrospective interviews, a handful of pop-up merch shops in Japan, and the release of *PaRappa the Rapper Remastered* for the PlayStation 4. I have played through every existing port of the game, but the *Remastered* port is the one I return to the most.

And it's almost impossible to read about *Remastered* without running head-first into two devastating words: *input lag*. In the spring of 2018, a user named KiiWii posted a bombshell to the message boards of GBATemp, a gaming community website. They had found that *Remastered* was essentially just an upscaled version of 2007's *PaRappa the Rapper* for the PlayStation portable (which was itself a rerelease for the game's tenth anniversary). Sony had developed an (admittedly pretty cool) method of turning the PS4 into an emulator that could automatically beef up the graphics of any ROM file it was designed to run.

All of that is fine—if the game played as well as it did in 1997. It does not. And that's because of lag that was already present in the PSP port, and imported uncorrected in the *Remastered* version. A flawed port of a flawed port is now the most common version of *PaRappa the Rapper*.

Like any space where many of its most vocal members are privileged enough to make an often-expensive boutique hobby the focal point of their lives, video game fandom is rife with overreactions to minor technical issues. From the "censorship" of Japanese games in North America to the distinction between "true" 1080p and an upscaled image, every aspect of the modern games industry serves as a potential battleground for gamers to unleash hell.

Kneejerk rage makes it hard to see whether a given complaint is legitimate. But if we sift through the ash of a thousand internet flame wars, it becomes clear that *PaRappa the Rapper*, and the entire rhythm genre that followed in its wake, are at risk of being lost in the translation of something both artistic and technical: their rhythm.

•

To explain why *PaRappa* and many other games experience input lag, I reached out to musician, sound designer, and independent game developer Matt Boch, who while at Harmonix took on key design roles for a variety of entries in the *Dance Central* and *Rock Band* franchises.

To process input commands, video games use what is called a *frame-dependent polling method*. "The fundamental digital technologies that underpin reproduction of sound and visuals are very frame-oriented," Boch explains. "And that frame cadence of 30, 60, 120, or 240? It essentially creates these tick-points along the timeline. So whatever our current frame rate is, we're only ever really doing the input processing (in most games) to resolve what happened in *that* frame."

Here's what that looks like. If a game is running at 60 frames per second (FPS), each frame is essentially a conversation between the processor running the game (let's say a PC or a console) and the input device (a keyboard or a controller). So, 60 times each second, the game is running a series of checks to see if it needs to send an updated frame. If the player pushes a jump button, the game will start the process of executing that command. If they push that button a millisecond after the 24th frame poll, they won't start to see visual feedback until the 25th frame poll confirms it.

But games are just programs following command hierarchies. If a lot of additional commands are being processed in that same poll (let's say, you want to jump, but also there are five enemies onscreen, and everyone is on fire), it could take more frames for your input command to register, or display on screen. Boch explains that when you add 16 milliseconds of this latency to the 5-to-16 milliseconds of latency that comes from a wireless controller, you can really feel the lag: "That's enough for me, as a musician, to not really feel like I'm playing or singing along with the track in the game."

For many games, this delay is acceptable. A half-millisecond delay is no issue when you're playing *Final Fantasy IV*, but it's the difference between victory and fatality when playing *Mortal Kombat II*. Rhythm action and music games like *PaRappa* base their entire experience around the player pressing a button in time with audio and visual cues. The feeling of *knowing* your timing was right, but the game telling you otherwise, makes a game feel unfair, unfun, and unplayable.

This is something Boch and their colleagues at Harmonix were sensitive to, and why they designed all of their PS2- and PS3-era games around *interrupt-driven input mechanisms*. With a polling-based system, delays can be exacerbated by the game having to process more requests on any given frame, and the player's input-command being bumped down the queue.

An interrupt-driven system, like the ones Harmonix built for their titles, instructs the game to give the player's input command priority over every other process—moving that one command to the front of the line. The "worst case scenario," as Boch puts it, of your command missing one frame poll and slipping into the next one, is minimized through this method. But it's far from industry standard.

Think of every step between you pressing a button and your monitor displaying that action in-game as a link in a chain. Old technology was a taut, short, chain. "The reason that your PS2 and PS1 controller ports have so many tiny, itty-bitty little holes, is that each one of those is a pin that connects to the chip that would read that controller, but that chip is inside a PlayStation," Boch explains. "When you push a button, it closes a circuit. And that's moving at the speed of light into the system." When paired with interrupt-driven technology, the command is sent, received, and acted on much faster than it could be via wireless controllers, or even controllers wired via USB.

Another link in the chain? Your monitor or TV. Cathode ray tube (CRT) displays worked by shooting electrons at a screen coated in phosphors. When the two collide, the phosphors get excited and glow; by shooting vertical lines of light across the screen many times per second, they could create a moving image. The amount of times per second the image is redrawn is measured in hertz (Hz), and is directly equivalent to the FPS rate. The standard broadcast frequency for most of the CRT era was 60 Hz, which meant most TVs were designed to display 60 FPS to meet industry standards. That same refresh rate requires significant processing power on modern, non-analog screens and monitors today.

"There's been work being done lately to try and develop technologies and HDMI protocols to minimize latency and to put TVs into automatic low-latency modes. None of those low-latency modes are lower than latency of a PS2, on a CRT television," says Boch. "None of them. Not a single one."

A game like *PaRappa the Rapper Remastered* faces input delay from the controller to the processor, more delay due to the processor's lack of a frame-dependent polling method, and still more delay if the ultimate output is being displayed on a laggy monitor or TV. These delays amount to fractions of a second, but they matter the most in moments where music games give the player full 1:1 control of input and feedback. From *PaRappa Remastered* to *Rock Band*, even non-musical people can sense on a basic level that they're not in sync with the game.

James Mielke highlighted these exact problems in the game, even in its original PS1 version. "If you're a really good *PaRappa* player and you're in sync, you're going to have that timing *down*. But if you're a guy just scrambling to keep up with what's happening on screen, you're just gonna sound *so* bad," he says. "*PaRappa* basically just exposed how bad your timing is."

All of these core issues were made even worse by flawed emulation in *PaRappa the Rapper Remastered*, which is trying to translate a system of input and timing commands three degrees removed from the hardware they were designed for. These problems are not new, and they're not even restricted to the world of music game developers.

During an interview with Kotaku at E3 2012, John Carmack, co-creator of *Doom*, spoke at length about the challenge of modern latency and lag problems. Comparing the leaps and bounds in internet data latency versus the problems with display monitors, he said that someone could send a packet of digital data "from the United States to Europe in less time than it takes to get a pixel out of the back of your computer into your display. [...] The only reason it's like that is because router and switch people know that latency is important; they give a damn about it, and they've done a good job with it. And display people aren't [there] yet."

Not every remaster or modern rhythm game suffers from input lag. The technology exists, on both the hardware and software, to reduce or eliminate the problems present in *PaRappa the Rapper Remastered* and many other precision-minded games on modern TVs. During our interview, James Mielke told me that quantization (a technique in music production where editing software locks musical notes into the exact time signature you're aiming for) could solve this problem on a genre-wide level. "Quantizing should help everywhere—it should be like the MSG of music rhythm games," he joked. "You should sprinkle it liberally and make sure it's on everything."

When it comes to hardware, HDTV monitors with CRT-level responsiveness are available, but are also prohibitively expensive. In the speedrunning community, where older games are common and every frame counts, playing on CRTs has become standard practice. The same goes for the classic fighting game community.

When asked about the prospect of a game like *PaRappa* being released today, Masaya Matsuura said he believes the industry is "not ready" for a game that lives and dies on input responsiveness. "Solution to the latency problem is not yet widely used," he told me. The almost-decade-long gap between Carmack's and Matsuura's comments is not an encouraging trend.

When I sat my wife down to watch me play *PaRappa Remastered* so she could understand why I'm willing to die for a rapping dog, I at least had a passable excuse for the many times I lost to the Chicken Level: This was a different game than the one I'd played 20 years ago.

Recreating the authentic experience so I can impress my spouse doesn't seem to be worth the time, money, and tech for the people making those calls.

In that regard, it's far from the only one. Hundreds of games exist in a place where they're only able to be experienced through their broken Special Editions.

But there were so many good ideas in *PaRappa* that they couldn't be denied. Not by Matsuura and Greenblat and the team at NanaOn-Sha, or by the many contemporaries that took the idea of a playable musical and ran with it.

And if we're going to accept that post-PaRappa music games owe various debts to rap's second most important doggfather, let's dig into what made *PaRappa the Rapper* so different in the first place: our hip hop hero himself.

PARAPPA THE RAPPER, TOO

LET'S RECAP: WE'RE now two-thirds through *PaRappa the Rapper*. PaRappa has gained all the skills he needs for his final battles. The last two levels fit neatly into what we recognize as normal challenges for a video game finale: a Boss Rush and a Final Battle. So before it all goes down, there's a single question worth asking.

Why is PaRappa a dog?

I turned eight years old in 1995, at the height of North America's love affair with *Mighty Morphin' Power Rangers,* a show that combined robots, karate, monsters, backflips, pyrotechnics, and public service messages that was basically lab-designed to dominate the waking hours of an ADHD kid. My brother and I were three years apart in age, and alternated years where one of us got to throw a party, so I'd had plenty of time to think of the *perfect theme*: Power Rangers.

Specifically, I wanted to theme the party around my favorite ranger, Tommy. The Green/White Ranger could summon a dragon by *playing a flute that was also a dagger*. He could also summon a *tiger*. In a show made entirely of superlatives, he managed to steal the spotlight. If anyone was going to get me Rangers-related merch, my preferences were well-documented: Tommy forever.

I walked away from my birthday with three Power Rangers toys from friends and family: three different action figures of the Black Ranger, Zack. Coincidentally (but not really), the Black Ranger was played by the only Black actor in the show. So why wouldn't he be my favorite?

Zack was a positive mentor to local children, he worked rapping and breakdancing into his fights, and I had never seen a Black person do martial arts before. But asking every Black kid in the world to see themselves in a single "teenager with attitude" goes back to that same problem with seeing yourself in the world around you. Black kids were given one mirror per show (if that), and we were expected to shut up and be happy with it.

If we're *not* happy about it, we make our own damn mirrors. If a character isn't explicitly one race, why can't they represent us? If we see ourselves in an alien, a monster, or a cartoon animal, who can say we were wrong?

I asked Rodney Greenblat and Masaya Matsuura why PaRappa was a dog, and they gave me the same behind-the-scenes answers that they've shared else-where: At first he was supposed to be a shrimp, but it was determined that a dog fit PaRappa's loyal and determined personality. In our email interview, Matsuura told me that "in the world of visual artistic expression (or the religious world, like Shinto), Japanese people (non-Japanese as well perhaps) can regard or see non-human characters as quasi-human; more easily so, when such characters behave like humans."

The human ability to connect emotionally to anthropomorphized creations is clearly nothing new. But I didn't just see "a person" when I looked at PaRappa. I saw a Black kid; I saw myself. And it made me happy.

I was afraid to ask PaRappa's own creators if PaRappa was Black, because I'm well-versed in the usual responses to these questions in the comment sections under my own articles: Does it matter? Does a dog, or a bear, or a *flower with a face* have a race? Those are examples of the types of questions people throw your way when the matter of representation exists solely as a thought experiment to them. Otherwise, they'd know the answer.

There are two ways to look at representation. The most literal one is a character that *looks like you do*. On this level, Zack *was* a good example of Black representation for me as a kid. So was Will (and the entire Banks family) from *The Fresh Prince of Bel-Air* (1990-1996),

Gerald from *Hey Arnold!* (1996-2004), and Bradley from *Stickin' Around* (1996-1998).[34] Those characters had the burden to stand in for *every Black viewer* in a way that White characters never have to.

The second type of representation offers a character that *makes you feel seen, even if they don't look like you.* This is the domain of headcanon: viewing non-human characters through extremely-personal racial lenses, a phenomenon that is totally commonplace among non-White people who needed to see more of themselves in the world around them. Unsurprisingly, I never saw my straight White friends practice this exercise (also sometimes called "racial drafting") as much as I did.

What does this look like? Let me show you a list of characters that are absolutely the same race as me:

- Max Goof (*Goof Troop, A Goofy Movie*)
- Piccolo Jr. (*Dragon Ball, Dragon Ball Z*)[35]
- Knuckles (*Sonic & Knuckles, Sonic Adventure*)[36]
- Both Bugs Bunny *and* Daffy Duck (*Looney Tunes, Space Jam*)
- Bob (*ReBoot*)

---

34   Here lies the most 90s Canadian Kid pop culture reference I will ever make.

35   "But to me, *Dragon Ball Z* also represents the journey of the black man in America." - RZA, *The Tao of Wu* (2009).

36   Some people were surprised when Idris Elba was cast as the voice of Knuckles in the second Sonic the Hedgehog movie. Not me.

- Simba and Mufasa but *not* Zazu (*The Lion King, The Lion King 1 ½*)[37]
- Optimus Prime (*Transformers, Beast Wars*)
- Goliath, Demona, and Broadway (*Gargoyles*)
- Plankton and Squidward (*SpongeBob Squarepants*)
- The Venom Symbiote (*Spider-Man: The Animated Series*)[38]

Any non-White second-generation child of immigrants who grew up in North American pop culture has a list like this in their back pocket—and everyone's list is different. My own brother's list is different from mine,[39] and we have the same parents. This list is how I gave myself permission to dream, and grow, and love things that didn't on their surface seem to love me back. And of course, that's how I saw myself in a dog named PaRappa.

If the creators and fans of the above works were to act like a certain British author of magical children's books and insist that certain diverse readings of their characters were *wrong*,[40] they couldn't stop me—or anyone else—from insisting that Knuckles's shoes clearly have the Jamaican flag's colors on them.

---

37 But not *Simba's Pride*.

38 But not Eddie Brock.

39 He thinks Sonic is Black, too. I'm just not there yet.

40 Expecto Patronizing.

Which is why these lists are often so personal, even if they're only maintained with a laugh and a smirk. Above all else, they're *hopeful*. When I pluck an unclaimed character out of the collective pop culture consciousness and say, "It looks like me," I see something great in them, and I wish that same greatness for myself. I feel a tiny bit less lonely in the world.

Most of my adult life has been spent trying to break into (and then out of) journalism. I love stories, fiction and nonfiction alike. And since I'm still in North America, I've always been a minority in every office and job interview I've stepped into. Sometimes I was the only person in an entire company who looked like me.[41] But this isn't about coworkers assuming I could dance, or asking me if I had seen *Black Panther* two weeks before it was released in theaters. It's about how a homogenous group sees the Other.

In the *Star Trek* franchise, entire alien species are treated as a monoculture, and if you understand the shape and customs of one Klingon or Ferengi, you know them all.[42] Once you realize how rampant this monocultural lens of the Other is across all genre fiction, it's easy to track it to other realms, from acclaimed dramas

41   "Handsome," is what I'm saying.

42   I'm fully aware that some of the best arcs in *Deep Space 9* and other entries in the franchise involve challenging or contradicting this mentality, but they're a latter-day amendment to a pervasive core problem.

to sitcoms. Hell, you can even find this idea buried deep in the fundamentals of journalism.

Stereotypes are a form of shorthand, a way to convey generalized information quickly and effectively. They have practical, everyday uses, especially when you're heading out of your comfort zone and want to know the basics of how to conduct yourself in a new environment. But they become the source of a way of viewing the world that resembles a game of broken telephone: Tons of racial and cultural stereotypes are perpetuated by individuals or groups who didn't have the time, energy, or inclination to verify if they're actually true. They're tall tales repeated with such confidence that they become the foundation of how so many people view the world around them. They're myths in need of some busting.

So while there is still validity to portraying some (for example) Black characters as tough-as-nails street-smart survivors of intergenerational poverty and the drug trade, it gets weird when that's *every Black character*. These characters will always exist alongside multiple characters of other races who span the spectrum of human experience. But the shorthand for being Black, or for what hip hop culture looks like, for *who you should be*, is so narrow.

And so you notice that Piccolo is the only one of his species, is widely misunderstood, and is an excellent father figure.[43] You see Max Goof feel embarrassed in his own body, at odds with his father Goofy's idea of family legacy, and electrified when he pretends to be Powerline, an R&B superstar. You internalize the lessons of Optimus Prime, who has to transform his true self to survive in the world, but never loses the courage and honor that make him a leader. Or at least that's what I did. But I wanted to ask around to see how other people looked for themselves in the art they loved.

Critic and journalist Gita Jackson first started playing *PaRappa* around the time of its release, alongside their older brother. From the very first cutscene of PaRappa and his friends hanging out in the fast food place, they saw something warmly familiar onscreen. "My dad and my brother had a certain cadence when they talked to each other; it was not the cadence that we use when we went out into White society, in a White world. [...] Sunny walks in, and just the way that [PaRappa is] talking about her and the entire design of that scene... It felt very familiar to me," Jackson says. "Not just in how I watched my older brother and his male friends hang out, but also in the ways that Blackness had been depicted in media at the time. It felt very *Fresh Prince*; it was about dudes getting up to mischief on their own."

---

43   There's a reason Goku's son, Gohan, wears a Piccolo-inspired fight outfit, and not Goku's gi, when fighting Cell.

The idea of warmth and normalcy permeates all of Jackson's observations of the game, from "making money to impress a girl," to an immediate interest in Kung Fu that had always existed in Black culture before being made explicit through the rise of the Wu-Tang Clan. But they also found an undercurrent of otherness, and latched onto it.

"Why does [PaRappa] assume Sunny doesn't want to go out with him? Oh, because: Look at this big popular dog [Joe Chin]. He's wearing a varsity sweater, and all these other aspects of Whiteness: He's got more money, he's got a nice car. It feels like they're deliberately trying to position this character within the narrative as an underdog, and that's just something that Black people really relate to."

The way Jackson talks about *PaRappa the Rapper* matches my own experience in many ways, including the fact that they repeatedly called the game "comforting." Today, the concept of cozy/comfy games is its own subgenre and aesthetic, and I love *Animal Crossing* as much as the next debt-drenched Millennial. But comfort, here, isn't coming from a cutesy art style or a relaxed gameplay loop. It's from familiarity and kindness that was *not* being offered in games at the time, and has barely happened since.

Outside of *PaRappa*, though, it was hard for them to find Black characters they related to, and Black femmes specifically. Being mixed-race complicated this even further; Jackson's parents were Black and Indian, just like mine. "Being confused about where I fit into the [Black] community [as a mixed-race person]... having non-human characters that felt Other to me, but weren't specifically Black, was always really, really helpful," they said. "*PaRappa* was an incredibly safe place for me to love and appreciate Black culture. And I didn't even realize that that was what I was doing! But it is such a soft and sweet love letter to Black culture in a way that did not make me feel like... I had to give up being Indian."

That binary doesn't exist when it's a world of talking dogs and teddy bears. "PaRappa? He's a little dog. He feels Black to me. He feels like he has something in common with me," says Jackson. "But that space and abstraction allowed me to feel more comfortable as a racialized person." (Carry that one in your pocket the next time someone asks *why representation matters*.)

Author, critic, and narrative designer Leigh Alexander told me about her journey through that process. "In my earliest memories of playing video games, they were all like: I was a little dude. *Bonk's Adventure*, Super Mario; I'm a weird little dude who jumps. I always picked the female characters, if there was one. But I don't think it ever occurred to me that it was a possibility that I would see myself. Or even now they've got Black hairstyles in video games, they still don't have *mine*, because I don't have amazing rows and dread-locks; I just have a busy head."

As she moved into the world of games journalism in the 2000s, her perspective on representation (or lack thereof) shifted alongside her.

"It feels bad for me to say—especially now because representation is so much of my work, and diversity is so much of my work. But like… it wasn't something important to me when I was young. And I think that's just because I never thought that it was possible," Alexander says. "And to some extent, you don't notice discrimination when it's everywhere, you just accept that it's the norm."

One of the more grounding things I've learned while putting this book together is how *specific* the drive to see yourself in your media of choice is, even among marginalized people. Everyone has a unique checklist of what they'd need to see and feel in order to be meaningfully represented. Both Leigh Alexander and James Mielke told me versions of the same idea: Since they had no reason to expect representation, they never really looked for it. Part of this could be chalked up to generational norms, privilege, or both; representation is a common concept when I talk to people my age or younger, but I've struggled to explain the concept to elder members of my family in the past.

If there is a universal argument for why representation matters, it can be found in the hard, circular logic of Alexander's words about looking back on her younger self: "I never thought that it was possible."

In the absence of a one-to-one representation of how she looked and felt, Alexander looked for broader ways to see herself in her player avatars. Women with big hair in *ElfQuest*. The brassy, unapologetic toughness of Rogue from X-Men. But when it came to games, she had to lean on different criteria.

"What verbs do they use that you can identify with? How do they perform themselves?" she says. "I think that [gameplay] mechanics can do a lot to characterize. Mechanics in narrative design do a lot to characterize, when the visuals don't."

PaRappa is a rapper because the gameplay allows him to rap. But what does a rapper look like?

•

PaRappa isn't a household name today, but he's not a total stranger, either. For various generational pop culture reasons that will only serve to make me feel incurably ancient, *PaRappa the Rapper 2* (released in North America in 2002 for the PlayStation 2, five years after the original) seems to be the game embraced by modern meme culture and streamers. But like many 90s-era mascots, he was lampooned by outside media. Most famously, the stop-motion animation sketch comedy show *Robot Chicken* featured PaRappa in a trio of skits throughout its ongoing history.

The first sketch features PaRappa snitching in court to get a plea deal, and it ends with him shot to death on the courtroom steps with an *immediate jump cut* to a joke about Notorious B.I.G.'s posthumous *Life After Death* album. The second one features 50 Cent, and once again ends with gunshots. His final appearance is a brief, homophobic joke. Adult Swim comedies helped me, like millions of others, find my weird comic voice. I'm under no illusions of pearl-clutching when jokes from twenty years ago don't hit like they used to. But it sucks to see a character you identify with reduced to the same cheap tropes that have been leveled at you your whole life.

PaRappa the Rapper was released in Japan three months after Tupac Shakur was murdered in a still-unsolved escalation of East Coast vs. West Coast rap-adjacent gang violence that all but transformed the mainstream view of hip hop as an art form and culture. By the time it was released in North America, Christopher "Biggie Smalls" Wallace a.k.a. the Notorious B.I.G had been murdered (his case also unsolved), and the tragic legend was complete. To the White observer, this *was* hip hop and rap culture. To the incurious and uninformed outsider, this was what a rapper looked like: a murdered Black man and a legacy of violence.

The idea of rappers being cursed to die young, violent deaths is in many ways an artifact of the mid-90s rap scene, frozen in time despite decades of progress. The most popular rappers alive today are fashion moguls and multi-hyphenate CEOs that are as safe and untouchable as anyone else in the Fortune 500 C-suite. But that handful of success stories doesn't change the fact that Black bodies keep the score, and the clock on that progress is reset with every young, violent death that turns a human being into a hashtag. For entire generations of rappers, the price they paid to turn stories of struggle into success was at the cost of their bodies: physical and mental trauma, addiction, and chronic health conditions.

It's a joke to the point of cliche that aging rock acts are trotted out to play the hits for decades past their 1970s peak; I make like six Aerosmith jokes in this book alone.[44] But it's also a common sight to see rockers on tour well past middle age, and even into their 60s and 70s. Their longevity becomes a cosmic reward for "making it" as a musician. And it's true for every genre except hip hop.

A lot of fans will never get to see a corny reunion tour of their favorite MC trying to hold the same swag

---

44 Will I go for seven? Dream on.

of their youth while performing in their 60s. I will never see Earl Simmons and Daniel Dumile perform as DMX or MF DOOM again. There will never be an equivalent of the Backstreet Boys Cruise for Run DMC, Wu-Tang Clan, or A Tribe Called Quest. It's a profound, creeping loss—of legacy, of a peaceful final act—that contributes to the grab bag of anxieties and fears that you carry around with you while Black.

There are J Dilla beats and DOOM verses (and vice versa) that still make me smile every time I hear them. And that's magic. That can't be taken away, even when the world takes them away from us. But with anyone on the spectrum of fame, I think there's an assumption that there will always be time later to reflect and respect what they've done for us. And as the absence of so many elder rappers can show us, that's not always the case.

Hip hop has its heroes, and they deserve their sunset years. But we can give them their flowers right now; if PaRappa represents anything, it's that joy belongs in hip hop as much as any other primal emotion. Not every celebration of a life needs to follow its conclusion. So if they don't know, let 'em know.

•

I love that *PaRappa* had zero interest or intent to engage with a limited, negative view of the art form and the culture surrounding it. It's why the game remains engaging and approachable to this day: It's a game about a rapper, free of the unkind, inaccurate cultural baggage that comes with the word.

Despite the fact that he was in one of the few hit games of the 1990s where you *can't hurt anyone*, PaRappa is used in jokes about real-world murders. And while his fans (old and new alike) know what he's about, PaRappa will always fight against the time-frozen idea of what a rapper looks like. Because what *PaRappa the Rapper* gives us is incompatible with a simple shorthand. A rapper can look like an onion, a chicken, a moose, or a frog. I could see myself in each of these animals (and one vegetable) without being corrected or reprimanded.

PaRappa isn't defined by what he does (rap), he's beloved because of who he is. And we can't talk about the final boss battles of his game until we establish what he's fighting for. It's reflected in the catchphrase he announces with fanfare and flourish before each of the first four levels begin. And it's the prize he's working for in the final two, when that catchphrase vanishes from his cutscene dialogue.

PaRappa isn't out to save Sunny Funny from a renegade villain and win her heart/a cake in the process.[45]

---

45   One year after Princess Peach baked Mario a cake to thank him for *freeing her from a shadow dimension inside of a living painting*, PaRappa baked a seafood cake for Sunny Funny to celebrate her birthday.

He never defeats and dominates rival Joe Chin. The final challenge of *PaRappa the Rapper* is about a teenager fighting to believe in himself.

GOOD ENOUGH

WHEN I ASKED RODNEY GREENBLAT about PaRappa's ongoing fight for self-confidence, he described those character traits as "human anxieties." Video games train us to fight off alien hordes, demonic invasions, and fabulously-dressed demigods.

What they don't teach us is how to live with ourselves. And that is the story of *PaRappa the Rapper*'s entire six-level, hourlong runtime. PaRappa is a kind, well-liked teen who spends half the game in his own head, daydreaming about a world in which he's better. He imagines being buff enough to fight off bullies, free enough to take a road trip in a flying car, rich enough to sweep Sunny off her feet, and a good enough baker to show up Joe Chin at her birthday party.

In my first playthroughs of *PaRappa* as a teen, I took each level to be a playable musical montage of PaRappa learning the skills to be better and save the day. Even back then, I understood that video games were power fantasies, and I used the visual shorthand of other underdog stories[46] to lump this one alongside movies like *The Karate Kid* and *Rocky*. If you watch enough of those stories, you walk away with two (possibly unintentional) lessons: that personal growth is easy, linear, and relatively quick, and that your value as a human being can be directly tied to your mastery of a talent or skill.

The core value of an underdog story is its optimism in the meritocracy we desperately want to see in the world around us. But in the power fantasies of many underdog tales, the protagonist not only improves but becomes an absolute *master*. By the end of many games, you aren't just a character, you are the *best person* in the entire universe. Each new generation of Pokémon games puts you into the shoes of a child so good at monster battles that they immediately become the world champion and end organized crime along the way. Samus Aran completes every Metroid adventure with the combined might of modern space science and multiple extinct alien cultures. Even if you start off an RPG as a Level 1 Chump of Humble Origins, you *will* be killing God with a sword before the end credits.

Your average underdog story is a Chosen One narrative with an added helping of bootstraps. The sad, solitary, and often *very relatable* starting points of these

---

46   Fun fact: PaRappa *is* a dog!

stories is just a launch pad for their heroes to end up becoming legends.

For most people, growth doesn't look like this. It's personal and hard-won and *important*, but it can often go ignored by the people around us. If we're trained to expect a parade and a freeze-frame-to-credits moment when we achieve a goal, the reward's absence can feel devastating. Not everyone expects the world to literally operate like a sports movie, but we do internalize the art we consume. We are what we eat.

So when I first played *PaRappa*, I thought I was playing an underdog story in the traditional sense. I was wrong.

At the start of each level, a cutscene sets up PaRappa's expectations of what personal growth will get him. They're cartoonish and exaggerated, but they're also not that far off from your traditional underdog story's happy ending. But at the end of each stage (or the start of the next one), we're shown the reality of all of these daydreams and expectations, and they're way more grounded than you'd expect from a cartoon about a canine teenager.

Stage 1 starts with two bullies harassing PaRappa, PJ, Katy, and Sunny while they're eating lunch. No one is ever in real danger; they're just being creeps. Joe Chin enters the scene and starts (literally) smothering the two creeps in question, and everyone but PaRappa leaves the restaurant. In his mind, the expectation is set up: If he were a "hero" like Joe Chin, he'd take out both bullies in a brawl and save the day. He seeks out Chop Chop Master Onion, and learns karate. But once the level is over, nothing happens. The scene is still in the restaurant, hours later, as Joe finally finishes his speech and the bullies collapse from the sheer weight of his monologue. They are *never seen or mentioned again*. PaRappa never actually harms another character.[47]

Stage 2 sets up PaRappa's expectation that getting his driver's license will open up a world of flying-car adventure. In reality, he trashes his dad's car in the opening cutscene of Stage 3 (while daydreaming about taking Sunny on an exotic vacation), and has to scramble to land a part-time job so he can pay to replace what he wrecked—and he does! Finally, Stage 4 sets up PaRappa's expectation that buying the perfect cake will earn him Sunny's affection, and after he drops it in the street, he needs to make a new dessert from scratch. (I guess you don't have a lot of cake cash lying around after buying your dad a brand new car.)

---

47   Okay, that's not true. In the Legally Distinct Version of Super Smash Bros. that is *PlayStation All-Stars Battle Royale* (2012), PaRappa appears as a playable character. He uses karate, his skateboard, and Boxy Boy as weapons. In an interview at the time, Rodney Greenblat said he was "not so happy about [PaRappa] being in a weapon-filled battle game."

All of the win states of these levels are normal, every-day outcomes where a teenage kid does his best to reconcile his (unrealistic, borderline unhealthy) expectations with the more mundane realities of how the world works. *I was that teen.* I thought I was one grand gesture away from winning someone's heart, one guitar lesson away from becoming a musical prodigy, or one snappy Aaron Sorkin-esque comeback away from silencing my bullies into oblivion. So of course I thought that was the story I was playing.

PaRappa never becomes a karate master, an expert driver, a rich flea market mogul, or a celebrity baker who dazzles his friends with his prowess. PaRappa's friends (Sunny included) already like him for who he is at the start of the game.

But the real stakes for each level are repeated through Stages 1 to 4, right before the gameplay begins: *I gotta believe.*

This game isn't a power fantasy; it's a story about being good enough. The player guides PaRappa through a handful of lessons so he can see the value in himself.

The idea that a story is only valid (or that a game is only good) if it focuses on the pursuit of perfection and mastery wasn't just something Masaya Matsuura had no interest in creating. In his view, it's a belief system that's antithetical to music itself.

To Matsuura, there is much more to art than simply mastering your craft on a technical level. He references artists like Picasso and Taro Okamoto as examples of people who pursued a creative vision that wasn't held back by expressions of pure technical skill. In his eyes, the world of music is far less willing to embrace the audio equivalent of a Picasso, and is subsequently missing out on new ways to enjoy and celebrate the art form.

This statement of intent to make room for "expressions beyond just being good" is most obviously showcased in the music changes for the various Rappin' rankings—BAD and AWFUL aren't punishments, and all of them keep a steady beat and let the player express themselves musically. But in a game as thoughtfully designed as *PaRappa the Rapper*, that core idea of failure being instructive necessarily carries through to the big finale, in terms of both narrative and gameplay.

PaRappa can learn the lessons and grow, but he needs to overcome the unrealistic expectations in his own head and *believe he's good enough* first. *PaRappa the Rapper* emphasizes non-toxic self-confidence: the ability to acknowledge and celebrate your own growth without the external proof of mastery/dominance over others that we've all been taught to expect when someone gets better at something. You've gotta *believe*, because you're the only one who can give yourself that validation.

So in a game where the enemies are situational bouts of anxiety and self-doubt, what does a final boss look like? What does a *happy ending* look like? Weirdly enough, it kind of looks like *Mega Man 2*. But first, we need to make a quick trip to the bathroom.

(C)RAP BATTLE

I WAS A TEENAGER when the movie *8 Mile* was released in the fall of 2003. It came out on home media a few months before my sixteenth birthday, and since it was another even-numbered birthday, I had a party. I still remember the silence and puberty-laced giggles as a dozen teens (and my Mom) sat around watching Eminem have sloppy, frantic sex with the late Brittany Murphy against a wall. But what really stuck with us as a society were the following cultural shifts:

1. "Lose Yourself" became the national anthem for all White People.[48]
2. Battle rap ascended to mainstream culture.

Like every other teenage boy I knew, I walked away from that film—a personal and powerfully small-scale retelling of Marshall Mathers's own coming-of-age story in the rap scene of Detroit—with one truth burning in

---

48   Wait for those opening piano and guitar riffs to hit at a crowded bar, and you'll see. It's like watching the tide come in.

my heart: *I totally could do that.*[49] The image of two rappers on stage, separated by an MC/referee, cannot be removed from the popular image of what a rapper looks like. But that image, as accurate and vital to the history of the culture as it is, may have become inflated over time.

Battle rapping as a subset of hip hop has a long and colorful history, and most hip hop heads can rattle off a list of their favorite battle rap verses and/or battles from the past few decades. Rap battles usually fall into one of two camps: completely improvised duels (as seen in *8 Mile*) or the more-common occasion of rappers going head-to-head using previously-prepared verses with improvised rebuttals thrown in at the start of each subsequent verse to acknowledge any heat that may have just been thrown their way.

Even though battle rap is a small slice of the culture, many of the most popular rappers of all time (especially from the East Coast) can attribute their style or lyrical pedigree to participating in battles. Battles are exciting, athletic spectacles of how quick a rapper's mind can work, and how flexible language can be as a platform and a weapon when a master gets on the mic.

Every notable battle rap feud from the 1980s until the mid-2000s is deserving of its own serialized podcast investigation and/or miniseries. Consider the

---

49 I totally could not.

"Roxanne Wars" of 1984-1985, where dozens of diss and/or answer tracks were produced around "Roxanne, Roxanne," a B-side by hip hop trio UTFO about a girl they wanted to hit on. It eventually spiraled out into an entire universe of songs featuring at least three young women rapping from the perspective of the (fictional) Roxanne, her family members, and other failed suitors.

A few years earlier in 1981, Kool Moe Dee vs. Busy Bee Starski signaled an immediate end of the gold school era of rap MCs, with Kool Moe Dee's lyrical, combative style completely washing away Starski's sing-song (and *PaRappa*-esque) feel-good hype rhymes in a dramatic changing of the guard. And of course, all battle rap feuds blend into the concept of Rap Beef, which gave us stories (and tragedies) like the murders of Tupac Shakur and Biggie Smalls, as well as decades-long hate feuds like Jay Z vs. Nas.[50]

The history and importance of battle rap is foundational, but increasingly obscure. The fine details have faded away, leaving us with only the outline: rap as a genre where two people angrily yell at each other until a murder eventually occurs. It's a view that isn't just inaccurate, it's depressing. Yet the battle rap in *PaRappa*

---

50   In "Takeover," Jay Z describes Nas's entire career as "a one-hot-album-every-ten-year average." I think about this verse regularly, and feel bad for Nas—a famous millionaire who was once married to Kelis—every single time.

the Rapper might be the best stage in the game. And as usual, it threads the needle by finding the universal constant in a very specific scenario: pooping.[51]

•

At the start of Stage 5, "Full Tank," all of PaRappa's metaphorical (and literal) chickens come home to roost. Sunny Funny's picnic birthday party is carried out successfully. Sunny and friends seem to be having a great time, and in the background we can see Joe Chin staggering around with his giant caketastrophe, before ultimately falling over. PaRappa eats multiple slices of Seafood Cake, a decision that will come back to haunt him later.

Eventually, Katy Kat pulls a move right out of the rom-com playbook and slyly leaves the party early with PJ Berri so PaRappa and Sunny can watch the sunset, alone together. His heart is beating so hard, it strains against the fabric of his shirt, *Looney Tunes*-style. And then the player is treated to a sound effect they've never heard before, as PaRappa's face contorts in horror.

It's somewhere between turntable scratching and a distorted guitar whammy bar, followed by the downwards wail of a sad trombone. It's played alongside an X-ray view of PaRappa's stomach, as we see its contents (shown as pink liquid) rapidly rush towards the bottom

---

51 *Everyone Poops*, Tarō Gomi, 1977.

of his digestive tract. "No, not now," he says, echoing the words of everyone who has ever lived. "I have to go to the bathroom!"

His mind flashes back, picture-in-picture style, to the multiple slices of Seafood Cake, and the sound effect plays again. He looks up to the sky to watch a flock of ducks flying by, and they turn into flapping toilets before his eyes. His face locks into a permanent scowl, and Sunny is *into it.* He's manly, stoic, and emotionally unavailable.[52] With literal hearts in her eyes, she asks him to drive her home. He hops in the car, and the sound effect/X-ray combo hits for a third time.

On the drive back into town, one of the few non-playable songs in the game starts blaring through the radio: "Love You RAP," a slow jam about feeling like you're "almost on fire." The musical notes floating out of the car's speakers turn into tiny floating toilets, because why not. In the city, PaRappa spots a gas station, mumbles an excuse, and rushes to the bathroom in a back alley. But there's a line of people waiting to use it, and he's almost out of time. "What can we do?" he asks the four shadowy figures ahead of him.

With a musical flourish and a literal spotlight appearing over each of their heads, the other people in line reveal themselves to be the *Four Rap Masters*. Chop Chop Master Onion, Instructor Mooselini, Prince

---

52   We don't have time to unpack all that—let's just keep going.

Fleaswallow, and Cheap Cheap the Cooking Chicken are between you and a public toilet. They present you with their final test, and the only logical solution: "Let's rap for it!" they all agree.

We take our bowels for granted. We don't remember how much of a gift and privilege it is to be able to control when we use the bathroom until that option is taken away from us in one way or another. And if you've ever shit your pants as an adult,[53] you're aware of the emotional rollercoaster that comes with using every ounce of your self-control to stop something from happening, and the mix of relief/horror once you can't hold it back anymore. You stop having one problem and immediately inherit a *much worse problem*.

It is also, objectively, hilarious. And this is the backdrop of *PaRappa*'s take on battle rap. The Rap Masters, your former teachers, offer no sense of menace or violence. But the stakes are real, both for the characters and the player. Like all the stages before it, this doesn't resemble any version of battle rapping that exists in our world; PaRappa continues to parrot back the same verses thrown at him, and he "wins" simply by not getting tongue tied and choking along the way. It's a war of attrition, and it's the player's final test heading into the finale.

---

53   Full disclosure: I have, in three continents.

Every video game teaches its audience how to play it, and good game design makes those lessons feel almost invisible. But there are times where those lessons crystallize into tests the player needs to pass in order to keep playing. There are a bunch of terms floating around to describe the various ways these tests manifest: skill checks, difficulty spikes, boss battles. But one that my brother and I have always associated with Japanese developer/publisher Capcom is the *boss rush*—or, as we call it to this day, "Pulling a Capcom."

These were made most famous in the Mega Man games for the NES, reaching the form we're all most familiar with in *Mega Man 2*. The core game consists of eight stages with eight Robot Masters at the end for the player to fight and defeat. But this is followed by a handful of levels where the player raids the evil Dr. Wily's castle. And right before that final fight, the player is thrown into a room with eight warp pads leading to rematches with the bosses they've defeated before, but now they all need to be vanquished one more time. It's a comprehensive prep exam, asking the player to repeat the skills they've demonstrated in rapid succession before heading to the finale.

Elements of a boss rush are present in countless Capcom-published action games, from *Devil May Cry* to *Viewtiful Joe*, and a dedicated Boss Rush mode is a common feature in many games. But it's still wild to see this play out in a cartoon rhythm action musical. Masaya Matsuura has said numerous times that he's not sure if he even views *PaRappa the Rapper* as a "game" in the traditional sense, but a boss rush is about the most game-y thing you could do with a penultimate stage.

The entire stage takes place in an adorably gritty back alley setting, with PaRappa facing each Rap Master in a quick quartet of verses before defeating them and moving one step closer to the bathroom door. Graffiti covers the cinderblock wall behind the characters, featuring family-friendly Greenblat tags like "THE HIP HOP HERO ZERO" and "DIAPER SERVICE." The sky's the color of a blood orange, and the beat is all tense guitars and funky synths. It feels like a *showdown*.

There's a lot to love in this stage, which quickly reminds the player that, as quick and poppy as the game is, there is care baked into every line of code. Each Rap Master opens up their lesson with a clever intro verse about how badly they need to use the toilet, and their playable verses are twists on lines from their dedicated levels, but more bathroom-themed. Master Onion talks about chopping down the bathroom door; Mooselini asks if you've checked the toilets on your right and left.

But even though the verses are familiar, the button combos are more complex than in their original stages. Mooselini's second pair of verses plays with the timing of her rhymes, despite having the exact same lyrics. By the time you reach Cheap Cheap, you're facing dense double-line stretches of button inputs that are the trickiest in the entire game. But it's familiar enough that a part of the player's brain will recognize the rhythms and cadence from her previous level and (hopefully) pull through.

Everybody in this level looks straight up *miserable*. PaRappa's face is tinged blue, he's squirming with concentration, and his eyes seem permanently glazed over with tears. All of the Rap Masters are in constant pain, and when they lose, their eyes turn into crosses and they jump offscreen, Dead Mario style.

Like every other stage in the game, the music and presentation shifts as your Rappin' level falls. When things are BAD, the tense sunset becomes a torrential rainstorm, and the level's beat becomes a drum track and a bass riff that sounds almost exactly like (but is legally distinct from) "Come Together" by the Beatles. Drop to AWFUL, and a sinister, almost industrial synth note joins the beat as a thunderstorm erupts above the alleyway. Fail the level entirely, and you get to experience my favorite game over screen in gaming history.

A trumpet-heavy salsa-flavored jingle starts to play as the camera zooms in on PaRappa's stomach via X-ray once more. Inside, *archival footage of a real rocket launch* plays, with neon-colored accents and action lines added for extra impact. The grainy shuttle detaches from its rocket, falls through an empty blue sky, and explodes. Subtlety is for cowards.

It's playful, memorable, and hilarious without being disgusting. When you consider that the level's backing track[54] is a mini-musical centered around characters yelling about their bowel movements, it's surprisingly clean and tasteful. It is the most punishing loss in the entire game, but only leaves PaRappa embarrassed, not dead. It is, in the realest sense, potty humor.

If the player clears all four Rap Masters, PaRappa noiselessly relieves himself on the toilet without a fart sound effect to be heard, sighs, "This is life," and flushes. Upon returning to the car, he's his smiling, bubbly self. And Sunny can't help but internally register her disappointment that the brooding hunk is now "the same old PaRappa" again.

The story, in terms of dialogue and stakes, ends at Stage 5. And it's hard for me to be mad at that. What realms does PaRappa have left to conquer, really? He got some spending money, he took Sunny out on a great birthday date, and he managed to avoid soiling himself in the process. PaRappa the Rapper is in a good place, and we helped get him there.

So there's only one thing left for him to do.

---

54   Which sounds a whole lot like "Fire Eater" by American rock band Three Dog Night.

YOU GOTTA DO WHAT?

PaRappa the Rapper doesn't save its hardest stage for last. Depending on your own abilities (and the version of the game you're playing), most people say The Chicken Level or the Bathroom Level gives them the most trouble. And on a narrative level, the final stage has nothing to do with the rest of the game. Even in terms of basic song composition, it sounds and plays very differently from every other track.

This isn't a final battle, a boss rush, or a gauntlet. This is PaRappa's Hip Hop Hero moment. It lasts just under four minutes, but he truly gets to feel like a rapper.

And so does the player. Stage 6 of PaRappa the Rapper is the titular character's playable theme song, and he raps it himself. He's ready. So are you.

After Stage 5 ends, all the cutscenes are wordless. Stage 6's opening cutscene plays more like a music video, or an end-of-movie montage. PaRappa receives a private invitation[55] from someone named "Rodney" to CLUB FUN, and he can bring one guest. He starts daydreaming about Sunny, and the rest is classic teenage stuff. Even though it's ostensibly a night out at an all-ages(?) club, it's all framed like Prom Night. We see shots of PaRappa and Sunny confirming their date over the phone, and both of them getting ready. PaRappa's Dad sees his son off, and PaRappa pulls up to Sunny's house (a giant lemon, because why not) with a flower in hand.

Her father (some sort of flower pot/military general) answers the door, and after giving PaRappa his stamp of approval (and accepting the flower for himself), PaRappa and Sunny are off to the club to be greeted by Katy Kat. The entire scene is backed by an original track, "Funny Luv," with vocals by Saundra Williams. It's earnest and sweet, and I forget it's in the game every time I reach the final level. As PaRappa and Sunny enter the club, Rodney Greenblat's creations fill the screen. Joe Chin wordlessly swaggers his way through the background beside a gigantic wind-up robot; a tattooed bulldog in a tank top that just reads "U.S. NAVY" gyrates beside a human chef. In the ebb and flow of the dancefloor, Sunny is swept away from PaRappa, who is bumped up against the main stage.

---

55   His full mailing address: PARAPPA RAPPA, 10 PETSHOP LANE, NEWFUNTOWN, NEWFUNLAND

As the backing track finishes, PaRappa is pulled onstage and the final level begins. PaRappa's theme song is about to be brought to life, and if you've been paying attention, you'll already know the hook.

•

One of the common sentiments Rodney Greenblat has expressed, both in previous interviews and when talking to me, was that PaRappa should have been a *star*. The Sony PlayStation was an unproven entity in the gaming world when the game was in development, and even members of the game's staff, like Ryu Watabe, didn't believe the PS1 could truly challenge the titans of the gaming industry, Nintendo and Sega.

Then *PaRappa* came along, and Sony had its own cool, family-friendly, cartoon mascot character. His debut game sold millions of copies while being an artistic anomaly, both then and now. He was simple enough in his visual design for a child to draw, but complex enough to be a fully-animated character in games, comics, cartoons, or movies. His game also served as its own companion soundtrack.

Sony took all of this momentum and promptly tried to make Crash Bandicoot their flagship mascot character instead.

It took Sony (and the character licensing industry as a whole) years to realize what they had on their hands with PaRappa. Hundreds of individual pieces of merchandise exist, and all of them have been approved by Greenblat himself.

There was even a short-lived, 30-episode *PaRappa the Rapper* anime that aired in 2001-2002. It was very much not approved by Greenblat himself (who was barred from contributing anything more than character designs), and is an inconsistently animated product that tried (and failed) to connect with young children. PaRappa raps *once* in the entire show—a single line, repeated for 30 seconds, in the final episode. An ill-advised spinoff is a rite of passage for any mascot character; he was in good company.

Despite the belated marketing push from Sony, PaRappa is no Mario. He's no Bugs Bunny. But he had all the same tools—including one that Mario took over a decade to find for himself. PaRappa had a *catchphrase*.

The first time it happens, right before Stage 1 begins, it's easy to dismiss it as a weird non-sequitur in a game composed almost entirely of delightful tangents. While contemplating how to stand up to his bullies, a lightbulb sparks in PaRappa's brain, and the music soars triumphantly as he says the line: "I gotta believe!"

But it continues as the only narrative constant through each new, wacky scenario. Driving test? "I gotta believe!" Part-time job? "I gotta believe!" The Chicken

Level? "I gotta believe!"[56] Like many other core elements of *PaRappa*, that catchphrase can trace its origins to one person: Ryu Watabe.

Before every other voice actor and singer joined the project, Watabe performed all the vocals for every track in the game—as well as all the cutscenes. In fact, the cutscenes were largely ad-libbed, with Watabe translating and interpreting Ito and Matsuura's Japanese script to English in one studio take. Matsuura would then edit those voice lines in time with the cutscenes, and that was that.

Because the entire final script essentially came from Watabe's translation, his final gift to *PaRappa* was especially personal: It was a phrase he had carried with him his whole life, a motto his high school football coach used to tell his team during tough games. In fact, he was going to use it as the title for his first album: *I Gotta Believe.*

"I think you've always got to keep a positive attitude in life, you know?" Watabe shared in the *PaRappa Guide Book* interview. "Many Japanese are so pessimistic and negative, so I thought, hey, they need this phrase, and I gave it to PaRappa," he added with a laugh.

It's so simple and earnest. It's a pep talk, an attitude adjustment, a mantra. It's a gift. And it's perfect.

---

56 But when you're about to poop your pants? NOTHING. Belief will not save you.

Less than a year later, the line was referenced and paraphrased with a knowing chuckle by the titular character of *Spyro the Dragon*. Every subsequent PaRappa appearance includes his catchphrase, from *PaRappa the Rapper 2* to *PlayStation All-Stars*. But it's more than that; this isn't just a prototypical version of "Bazinga," after all. It's the entire soul of *PaRappa the Rapper* in a single three-word phrase. "Believe in yourself" isn't exactly a novel nugget of wisdom, but when the dog says it, you believe *him*.

So when Stage 6 begins properly, PaRappa is center stage. The four Rap Masters (after a shower and a collective change of clothes, right?) dance behind him, serving as his hype team and backup singers. The song starts, and it sounds… like an actual *song*.

The backdrop is his own name and title, writ large. The camera zooms in, and we can see PJ Berri at the back of the venue, hard at work at his turntables.[57] The opening notes of a piano riff that has a legally-distinct similarity to "December, 1963 (Oh, What a Night)" by the Four Seasons kick in as MC King Kong Mushi[58] appears: a giant, four-armed insect hype man with dreads. Directly behind PaRappa, all four Rap Masters sway to the beat. Mushi starts vibing with the crowd,

57 DJ PJ. Get it?
58 Like some of the other Rap Masters, I only learned his name by reading the instruction manual.

kicking off a classic call-and-response ("Somebody say ho! Say ho ho!"), and then it happens.

The Rap Masters start to sing. They sing the only chorus in the entire game.

Whatcha gonna do when they come?

As always, we're shown the button prompts with the Rap Master's face as a cursor as a preview, before it switches to PaRappa's face when it's the player's turn. But the prompts don't match the rhythm of that line: Two [O] button prompts, emphasizing the "*gonna do*." And then another first is thrown at the player: PaRappa speaks for himself.

I gotta redeem!

We have a hook. We have non-repeated lyrics. We have a concert vibe. We are performing a *song*. And it moves quickly, part victory lap and part theme song.

Whatcha gonna do when they come? (I gotta relieve!)
Whatcha gonna do when they come? (I gotta receive!)

The Rap Masters, singing in a bright, church-choir style group harmony, end the chorus as they repeat their final question.

You gotta do what? You gotta do what?

PaRappa (and you, the player) respond with the only answer. He practically screams the words.

I gotta BELIEVE!!59

---

59   The in-game text uses two exclamation marks and all caps. I strive for accuracy.

The entire game has been building up to this one moment, and it's exactly as powerful now as it was when I first played it.

Verse 2 begins, and Mushi immediately starts dropping dense, two-line rhymes for the player to follow. But as with the hook, your responses are no longer just a playback of the lyrics you just heard. It's the only track in the game that could be passed off as a forgotten old school hip hop track from a mid-80s party album.

Hey yo everybody, just check out the way I live everybody!

(Yo yo Dverybody. It's the time you've been waiting for, here's the party!)

That being said, the illusion isn't perfect. The lyrics quickly veer into cheery nonsense, regularly employing turns of phrase that weren't a thing then, and certainly aren't now. Take the next verse, for example.

O, oh! O, oh! Here comes the dude, and now he's running up and down the street with the juice!

(Sunny's my life, She's like a dice, I cannot tell which way she'll turn till I spice!)

The lines are hot nonsense, but it's adorable and inspiring to watch PaRappa step out of the lyrical shadow of his teachers, doing his own thing. An hour earlier, you were helping him learn beginner karate moves; now he's freestyling his truth in front of a crowd. It feels *good*.

There are no goofy consequences for your Rappin' rank falling—the crowd and stage lights are cut and the backing track is diminished as you go from BAD to AWFUL, until you're left with just one Rap Master (Prince Fleaswallow) reciting the interlude, and a lone woman (Saundra Williams/Instructor Mooselini once again) singing the hook over a beat and a synth bassline. If you fail outright, PaRappa is left alone onstage, while Sunny gently tells him "Maybe next time!" after the track cuts out.

But there's no narrative risk, no ultimate prize. PaRappa is at a concert, performing a song made for him, and he needs to do well. It's remarkably low stakes, but also the most important thing that could happen to a teenager. (It's also, beat-for-beat, the emotional climax of 1995's *A Goofy Movie*, in which Max Goof—who is definitely Black—joins his musical idol onstage to showcase his own worth in a public way and impress the girl of his dreams.)

So the song continues, supported by your teachers, the Rap Masters, each prompting PaRappa to shout out the life lessons he picked up from each of them.

At last we enter Lesson 4—the final verse in the game.

It also breaks the whole damn thing in half.

Up to this point, every set of verses and button commands took place across two lines, and the player was given a chance to see and memorize them before they had to input them for real. The final lesson abandons the Simon Says format: PaRappa takes no prompts, and repeats the call-and-response crowd chant that King Kong Mushi opened the song with.

The problem is that since there's no demo phase for the player, you have no chance to see what's coming before you have to press the right buttons. And this is *extra* complicated because the next lines of inputs don't scroll into view; they're swapped out completely at the end of a line, like a page of sheet music being flipped by an invisible hand.

What's *supposed* to happen is PaRappa ends his own theme song by becoming his own hype man, supplanting the MC, and sending the crowd off on a high note.

What almost *always happens* to new players (and me, still, to this day) is that they run into an unprompted string of nine consecutive lines of button prompts that they cannot prepare for, and either end up rapidly failing the level or whiffing the final triumphant line. That last one is especially haunting, because PaRappa's *"Now screeeeam!"* line to the audience becomes him saying *"Now,"* followed by *absolute silence* as he chokes on his final word, and stares blankly into the crowd with a smile on his face.

I can't think of a better example of what *PaRappa the Rapper* really is than that frustrating and hilarious moment: A genuinely moving and effective fusion of music and gameplay that can be completely broken and warped into a surreal moment of player-generated comedy if you press the wrong/right buttons. That line rhyming "dice" with "spice"? It can just as easily become PaRappa yelling the word "Sunny" eleven times in a row with that same smile on his face.

The issue of new lines being unreadable for players was solved in *Um Jammer Lammy*, with each new line scrolling smoothly into view with clearly color-coded lines between NPC and player. It's the difference between scrolling down a block of text on a screen instead of turning a page in a physical book. All three games in the main PaRappa franchise are extremely similar on a mechanical level, but small quality-of-life changes like that demonstrate the difference between creative choices and universally-recognized problem areas.

Whether you completely bomb the final line and start over or nail it on your first attempt, that's the last playable verse in the game. PaRappa lands some lines of crowd banter, drops his catchphrase one last time...

...and that's it. The camera pulls back to a shot mirroring the one that opened up Stage 6, and the scene fades to a loading screen over the sound of applause. The final cutscene of the game echoes the first one, with the whole crew walking into a movie theater in the final moments of a film, with "THE END" plastered across the screen as they take their seats.[60]

The in-game credits roll while "Love You RAP" plays in its entirety, and then you're booted back to the title screen. If it was your first playthrough and The Chicken Level kicked your ass, it probably took you somewhere between one and two hours to finish the game. What comes next is up to you, and this is where people (myself included) may have failed to meet *PaRappa the Rapper* on its own aspirational terms.

I've described the game as a toy and a drum machine, and I use those terms intentionally. I sincerely believe that Masaya Matsuura and the entire team at NanaOn-Sha expected players to approach PaRappa as an endlessly-replayable musical world to return to in perpetuity. We had been taught all the basic chords; we had finished our tutorial. The rest was on us to explore and create.

For years, I saw *PaRappa* as a storybook. But after you beat each stage once, it secretly becomes a sandbox, and I didn't realize this until I started research for this book. What happens when an audience misses the core concept of a work of art? What happens when almost

---

60   The final shot of the movie seems to be footage of PaRappa driving his Dad's car away from his house and towards the horizon as his Dad screams and jumps on the sidewalk in protest. It's just layers on layers, here.

every derivative work inspired by the original focuses on the *exact opposite values* its creator wanted to embrace?

The honest answer is "The subsequent twenty-plus years of gaming history." But there's no better example of the gulf between creator intent and player reception than the weirdest, wildest, part of the game: Cool Mode.

TRANSLATING COOL

To CLEAR THE MAIN story of PaRappa, players need to complete all six stages with a GOOD ranking. The entire time, the potential of a COOL ranking is onscreen in grayed-out text that always seems beyond your grasp. That's because it is: You can't enable Cool Mode on a stage until you've cleared it once before, so most players will likely finish their entire first runthrough of the game before they even see the Stage Select screen, buried in the Options menu, which lets you skip the story and jump right into the gameplay.

Once you return to a cleared stage—let's say Chop Chop Master Onion, for example—performing a line perfectly while Rappin' GOOD will make the word Cool start flashing, as if you were about to get bumped up one level. But if you hit your commands perfectly, the prompt will vanish. Rinse and repeat. Perfect play will get you hints of Cool Mode, but you'll never actually achieve it. This haunted me for *decades*.

I have cleared *PaRappa the Rapper* and its sequels dozens of times throughout my life, and I had never reliably entered Cool Mode under my own power until a few months ago. The manual for *PaRappa* alludes to a "Master Course" and tells the player to follow their "own rhythm" while ignoring the score, but that wasn't nearly enough for me to work with, and I always got discouraged and moved on. I had pulled up YouTube clips of other players pulling them off, and wondered how they made it happen. Now, I've gone straight to the source.

Masaya Matsuura gave me a detailed breakdown of how Cool Mode works. "*PaRappa* has a clear scoring logic of evaluation based on the combination of a pair of sixteenth notes," said Matsuura. "It is 'rest,' or the absence of a sound, which gives the highest score. To get your 'rest' counted the highest, the remaining combination and variation should be played within the given timeframe."

When evaluating a player's input for Cool Mode, it's like the old saying about jazz; it's the notes you don't play that count. The dots and stars at the top of the screen generally break each bar into measures. Each star is a beat in 4/4 time, and each dot is a 16th note. The idea is to experiment with button presses outside of the mandatory ones dictated on each line, with a rhythm that still adheres to the placement of 16th notes.

Matsuura suggested I seek out the various online guides specifically for Cool Mode that have popped up over the years. I did, and they helped. But I also started to find far more message board threads from players who couldn't crack the code with any consistency. Then I watched Cool Mode streaming playthroughs where hosts shared their key secret: button mashing. This technique often tricks the game into giving you a pass.

That was how I finally managed to pull off Cool Mode in every stage except The Chicken Level. Once I completed a line in perfect time with instructions and had Cool flashing, the game urged me to use the notes on a given line as individual instruments to play around with while staying on beat. I could reliably enter Cool Mode by turning Master Onion's single-word *"Chop"* command into a stuttering *"Chop Ch-Chop Chop Chop"* input alongside the level's drum beat.

Still, button mashing is essentially leaving it up to chance. If you want to get into Cool Mode and stay there, you need to work within the standards of music theory. You can either trial-and-error your own personal rhythm for each stage, or you can pull up one of several existing guides (the one I found on GameFAQs was written in December 2000 by a user named ruyeyama) that give you peer-reviewed button combos and exact directions on when to use them to enable Cool Mode.

And when you do, *the game explodes.*

The visual and audio changes that signify BAD and AWFUL ratings are nothing like Cool Mode, because there's one other major change that comes along with it: the level's Rap Master leaves and takes the rapping cursor and icons with them.

Once you get Cool Mode in Stage 1, Master Onion mutters that he'll "lose money with students like you" and then *kicks away the walls and ceiling of his dojo* before flying into the sky. The rest of the stage has PaRappa alone in the now-flattened classroom in front of a blood-red sunset and mountain vista straight out of a Japanese woodblock print. The now-gigantic figure of Chop Chop Master Onion stands behind the mountains, watching you serenely. But you still have to keep playing to retain your Cool status.

This is where PaRappa lays its drum machine programming bare. The four face buttons and two shoulder buttons give you access to every voice line PaRappa can use in a level; hitting the same button in a row will play all the voice samples in that stack (press [✗] three times in a row on Stage 4 to say *"Crack crack crack"*), while holding down the left directional button will lock the voice samples to the "top" of each stack.

All these inputs still need to adhere to a basic rhythm and structure of the song's time signature. If you press the same button dozens of times or fail to enter any inputs at all, your ranking will drop back down to GOOD, and the Rap Master will gently chide your performance and continue the level from the closest relevant verse in the song's runtime.

Cool Mode changes more than I ever realized. Finishing each level with a COOL ranking leads to unique dialogue from your Rap Master.[61] Each level has something weird and playful happen, with the standouts being Stage 1, Stage 2 (your car rips in half, lifting a screaming Instructor Mooselini into the air like a parasail), and Stage 5 (the world melts away as PaRappa chases a golden toilet down a railroad track while rainbow colors swirl around him). In the final level, Chop Chop Master Onion starts breakdancing onstage if you keep Cool Mode going for long enough.

Even the post-credit cutscenes change if you finish a stage during Cool Mode, with little touches like PaRappa buying his dad an even more expensive sports car, or him being able to take a driver's license photo that doesn't capture him mid-sneeze. Clearing all six stages in Cool Mode adds a post-credits stinger promising "PaRappa the Rapper 2," and unlocks a minigame in which Sunny and KT dance for a crowd to an

---

61   They all feature your Rap Master being extremely positive and supportive—true to her brand, Cheap Cheap takes the opportunity to try and sell PaRappa her newest product, a Cherry Cake (only $19.95).

original song while the player can rotate the camera and change their outfits. It's weird, but it's there.

Finishing the main story of *PaRappa* as a video game gives the player access to *PaRappa* as a musical instrument. Cool Mode turns each stage into a visually-stunning music video where the tempo and order of the lyrics are entirely in the player's hands.

But I had to get direct coaching from the game's creator to learn about this feature in the proper light. How many fans explored the game to its full potential when it was first released? This opaque approach to a major aspect of gameplay was a failure of translation that has made it increasingly hard for audiences to experience the game as it was originally intended.

•

If you read enough articles about Masaya Matsuura, or simply talk to people who have worked alongside him, the word "genius" inevitably comes up. Rodney Greenblat said it, unprompted, multiple times. When we celebrate someone as a genius, we're often recognizing their ability to look at the same world the rest of us live in and imagine something better. To answer a question no one had thought to ask. But when you're always looking beyond the horizon, it's possible to lose sight of where everyone else is headed.

With greater insight into how Matsuura views musical expression on a fundamental level, I understand more of what *PaRappa the Rapper* was intended to be. And I also understand why video game fans were destined to fall short of interacting with his work in the way he had hoped for.

When trying to explain the type of music he felt was undervalued by society at large, Matsuura sent me a link to a YouTube video from 2009. It's an audio-only recording of an experimental UK-based orchestra called Portsmouth Sinfonia performing their 1974 rendition of "Also Sprach Zarathustra" by Richard Strauss, a.k.a. the song from *2001: A Space Odyssey*, a.k.a. Ric Flair's theme.

They are *terrible*, and purposefully so. Their whole deal was to gather trained musicians and make them play instruments they had never used before.

The "popular song but played badly on the wrong instrument" subgenre of internet comedy is a personal favorite of mine. I think the 20th Century Fox fanfare covered on a recorder will make me laugh until the day I die. So I was surprised, and delighted, when Matsuura essentially told me the world needed more of that.

"I know there are a lot of fascinating types of music that may not be skillfully played […] but embody attractive expressions beyond just being 'good,'" he said. He talked about times in his career with PSY·S where he felt limited by the fact that once a song was recorded to an album, any future listeners had only one way to experience it. He wanted to give them options.

"Isn't it better to offer people the opportunities to listen to the music as they want, or participate in music by introducing functions such as mods or customization tools, within the specified scope (to maintain the integrity of the work)?" Wouldn't musicians want to give their audience the tools to celebrate their music by creating their own?

This train of thought is what drove him to create *PaRappa the Rapper*—an experience where a player could customize an existing song in real-time to their own parameters without the need for technical perfection. The signs of this creative approach are everywhere, from the surprisingly robust freestyle controls in Cool Mode, to the fact that every song is perfectly listenable from its COOL to AWFUL versions. Hell, the seldom-discussed "Save Replay" function makes more sense when you imagine a world where friends proudly showcase their unique interpretations of a level's performance, with no two people freestyling or matching PaRappa's words to a level's rhythm in the exact same way.

In Cool Mode, we can see the truest expression of what Matsuura wanted players to feel: empowered to create music with an existing framework without having to worry about perfect performance or a Rap Master judging them for coloring outside of the lines.

The choice, for most players, is between doing the bare minimum to achieve their result, or embracing the possibility of open-ended, self-directed play. Some of the biggest games in history, from *The Sims* to *Minecraft*, have found massive audiences by giving their players a sandbox and letting them do the rest. *PaRappa* was already so unprecedented in so many ways, that its New Game+ turn as a freeform art-and-music generator went over a lot of peoples' heads, mine included. But even if that part of the game was clearly advertised from its opening moments, I doubt it would've made a difference.

Gaming takes a specific mindset for you to want to create your *own* art within a game. For every aspiring composer who crafted entire songs in *Mario Paint*, there were kids like me who were there to play the "Gnat Attack" minigame. It's hard to not see *PaRappa* as an unbelievably optimistic statement of intent—a belief that its fans will love and understand it for its surface level joys as well as its deeper mechanics. If nothing else, I hope it can be better understood today, and that a new generation of creators can create and share some Cool Mode compositions that let the world see the game as the toylike instrument it was created to be.

But there is a playfulness and an optimism at the core of *PaRappa* that shines through no matter how COOL you are. Like Matsuura said, imperfect art still has everything it needs to move us. And in one sentence, PaRappa tells us all he wants us to know.

I GOTTA BELIEVE!!

THREE WORDS. ONE catchphrase. I think that's what has saved PaRappa from the same landfill of So-90s-It-Hurts mascots like Gex, Bubsy, and Cool Spot. One of the best episodes of *The Simpsons* is about the introduction of Poochie, a rapping dog, to the long-running *Itchy and Scratchy Show* cartoon, as a spoof of the way out-of-touch corporations cynically mandate the creation of "cool" new characters to prop up ratings and sales.[62] Despite their surface similarities, Poochie is everything PaRappa isn't: hackneyed, insincere, and designed-by-committee.

At every opportunity, the *PaRappa* team chose sincerity. He raps because Masaya Matsuura and Rodney Greenblat believed it suited the gameplay and character they had in mind. The visual style is borne from the singular vision of a lifelong creator who rose to the challenge. The vocal performances come from a place

---

62   The episode aired about three months after *PaRappa* was released in Japan, and nine months before it arrived in North America.

of passion, talent, and play. While every other game involving hip hop in the 1990s and 2000s treats the genre as mandatory set dressing needed to exploit an untapped demographic, Matsuura's beats, Ryu Watabe's lyrics, and Gabin Ito's story show a love and respect for the art and culture of hip hop in broad, wholesome strokes.

PaRappa the Rapper was a game made by artists who gave a shit. It sold millions. And yet, paradoxically, it still feels like it wasn't enough.[63] Its history is a crash course in the game industry's shifting priorities, and maybe it says something about us players as well.

Greenblat and Matsuura both describe the aftermath of *PaRappa*'s success as overwhelming, but in different ways. The former admits that he wanted to move full steam ahead on a sequel, to strike while the iron was hot. But a lot more attention was now focused on Matsuura and NanaOn-Sha, both from the industry at large and (more critically) within Sony as a whole. Matsuura describes being overwhelmed by "a huge tsunami of feedback." Suddenly, the kitchen had too many cooks.

According to past interviews, the team was convinced to move away from rap music—it was seen by

---

63   Not to get stuck on this, but if we include *Um Jammer Lammy*, there were three games total in the PaRappa franchise. Cool Spot had four.

some people as a flash-in-the-pan musical trend ("like Ricky Martin," Matsuura told IGN in 1999), which Greenblat disagreed with. They instead pivoted towards a spinoff with a new character and a rock focus, which Greenblat wanted to specify more clearly as goth (and was voted down). The resulting game, *Um Jammer Lammy*, had a worldwide rolling release to PS1 across the spring and summer of 1999.

I loved *Um Jammer Lammy*. Of the three PaRappa games, I probably played it the most. It's weird and sloppy, and it trades the slice-of-life self-affirmation of *PaRappa* for something louder and more psychedelic. But I also can't defend it from any of its criticism. *Lammy* keeps *PaRappa*'s call-and-response gameplay structure, but now instead of repeating your teacher's words back at them, you play a guitar riff-repeat of a spoken word line. It's somehow even less like rock music than *PaRappa* was like rap music.

Most alarmingly, *Lammy* was subject to a major case of honest-to-God *censorship*. In the Japanese and European versions, the penultimate level of the story finds Lammy slipping on a banana peel (dropped by PJ Berri, a canonical murderer?) and *fucking dying*. She is called upon to support an idol in a *Hell concert for demons* to win her soul back. It's weird and funny and leads to the funniest gag in the entire series, where

Lammy realizes she's dead, only for the end credits to start rolling as she accepts her Game Over. It's dope!

In the North American release, this is all scrubbed away. No death, no references to Hell, and a few other minor-but-confusing changes to cutscenes or lyrics sprinkled throughout. Instead of dying, Lammy catches her belt on a doorknob and is flung backwards through time, landing in a jungle, where she (now in camo gear for no reason) is ushered onstage to the idol's concert.

A new cutscene, with dialogue and a lot of new CG to match, needed to be rolled out for one of the game's three regions. Greenblat confirmed to me that it was really an unexpected dash on his team's end when higher-ups at Sony dictated they change a finished story.

At the same time, *PaRappa*'s most popular features had already been digested and replicated by another titan of Japanese gaming: Konami. There's no record of Konami executives formally announcing their plans to make an arcade franchise using the core gameplay concepts introduced by *PaRappa the Rapper*—in business parlance, that's generally considered a "bad move"—but the calendar suggests it was likely a big influence.

When *PaRappa* was released in Japan near the end of 1996, Konami had zero music games in development. By the time *Um Jammer Lammy* celebrated its North American launch in 1999, Konami's Bemani arcade franchise was a household name in Japan.

Beatmania, the flagship title (and the franchise's ongoing namesake), hit Japanese arcades in late 1997, and used a peripheral that combined keyboard keys and a turntable to mimic the experience of DJing a live set for a crowd. By mid-1999, five versions had been released to arcades.

Dance Dance Revolution, or *DDR*, is the breakout international hit of the Bemani franchise, and became an immediately-recognizable culture touchstone in a way that *PaRappa* never could. Its first entry was released in September 1998, and to this day *DDR* remains the best way to have my validity as a human being absolutely demolished in real time. It's easy to draw a line from the high-adrenaline performance highs of *DDR* and its Bemani cousins GITADORA[64] to *Guitar Hero* and *Rock Band.* The rest is rhythm music history.

Every rhythm game that followed *PaRappa* would quickly eclipse it in terms of short- and long-term popularity and success, despite its initial influence on the industry at large. But that type of influence can endure long after its source has stepped out of the spotlight. Like a one-hit wonder immortalized as a perfect hip hop sample.

•

---

64   Which is somehow a contraction for "*GuitarFreaks & DrumMania*" in the same way "Pokémon" is a short form of "Pocket Monsters."

As the theory of the 30-year pop culture cycle predicted, we in 2023 are living in the 90s renaissance; a sequel to *Space Jam* has come and gone, and lofi hip hop music has emerged as a hazy recontextualization of a specific type of privileged 90s nostalgia. It's in this space where you'll find modern games that carry, implicitly or explicitly, the DNA and values of *PaRappa the Rapper*.

Simogo's *Sayonara Wild Hearts*, a "playable pop album" featuring Queen Latifah as the narrator, launched to rave reviews in 2019. The cult popularity of Newgrounds flash game *Friday Night Funkin'* contributed to its massive $2.2 million Kickstarter success in 2021 when its creator angled to expand it into a full release. And smaller-scale wins, like D-Cell Games' *UNBEATABLE* getting funding at $250,000, suggest an audience for narrative-driven, music-based games that the wider games industry seems uninterested in pursuing.

But it was Matt Boch, already a key part of many games in this abridged history, who helped me see what the next chapter of this subgenre could look like. "There's a fundamental linkage between that history of music visualization, and concert visuals and laser light shows," Boch told me. "It all has its whole own cultural discourse [outside of video games]."

You only need to play *Rez Infinite* or *Tetris Effect* to see Boch's vision in action; games that use music as part of a sensory experience that uses emotion and spectacle to connect with the player, rather than relying on timed button presses. Games that are less about performing music, and more about experiencing it.

The concept of "music games" is absurdly broad, when you say it out loud. Doesn't the name suggest that music games are about *all* music across every genre? The best ones self-select their focus through their names (*Rock Band*), but many more still go far too broad to be useful (*Guitar Hero* means… any song with guitars?). Boch believes more hyper-specific music games will be able to build meaningful gameplay around the strengths of their chosen genre. And that's true: *Rez* and the aforementioned *Wild Hearts* are focused and coherent because they stick to trance and synth-pop songs, respectively.

Can *PaRappa* take credit for all of these games, from *Guitar Hero* to *Get On Da Mic*? No, of course not. But the simple action of hitting buttons in time to music to feel things hadn't been made as fun, resonant, and *joyful* as it was when we first saw PaRappa leap onto our screens. And sometimes, all it takes is one example that something *can* be done before you allow yourself to believe you could do it, too.

When I asked Matsuura which modern games, if any, best represented what he was going for with *PaRappa the Rapper,* his answer surprised me. He said

Simply Piano, by JoyTunes, could be considered a "distant relative" to *PaRappa*. The game is a music teaching tool that you place nearby while playing your piano or keyboard; it uses your mobile device's microphone to pick up your note and guide your progress through what's essentially a gamified series of piano lessons.

I wish I believed in myself the way Matsuura believes in players. His goal from day one was to offer a playable music experience that didn't just teach us to repeat a pattern, but ultimately empowered us to express ourselves. What better form of play is there than the limitless potential of musical literacy? *Simply Piano* doesn't let players pretend to be Chopin, Alicia Keys, Lang Lang, or any other famous pianist. It lets you be yourself, getting better at an art form.

There is so much potential in programs like *Simply Piano* (or *Rocksmith*, Ubisoft's surprisingly durable guitar-teaching series), which make learning approachable and fun. I understand why Matsuura, the multi-hyphenate creator, wants a world full of new musicians to be allowed to flourish.

But even the ideal audience might have failed to see Matsuura's game on his preferred terms. *PaRappa the Rapper* is a musical, not a music lesson. People can immediately connect with its charm, heart, and whimsy; but on the flipside, I spent several hundred words trying to explain how Cool Mode works. As a musical,

PaRappa still isn't an easy candidate for flagship franchise appeal, because of that same earnest whimsy. Like many musicals, there is an undeniable silliness there, and it takes a specific frame of mind to allow yourself to connect with that.

Even as a late-90s video game, *PaRappa* stands out. At the exact same time players could watch a dog in an orange hat sing about the importance of believing in himself, they could have been embroiled in the cyberpunk seriousness of *Final Fantasy VII* or beating people to death in *Tekken 2*. You have to be willing to meet a musical on its own terms, and fewer games today ask that of their players. Fewer still dared to ship a product that offers less than 60 minutes of game time—the dollars-to-minutes ratio has crept into almost every major game released in the past decade, and we're living in its end result.

The same types of people who, ten years ago, were complaining that games like *Plants vs. Zombies* and *Superbrothers: Sword & Sworcery EP* were too expensive by daring to charge more than $0.99 on the App Store are the same ones being targeted by marketing campaigns boasting how many *hundreds of hours* a game takes to complete. It is a shift in core values that leaves little to no room for the experiences and challenges a game like *PaRappa* can offer as a work of art. And what it offers is an alternative to every other power fantasy or epic struggle you can play today: it tells us that we're good enough as we are. All we have to do is believe the story.

The reason we tell ourselves stories of hard times is simple. They serve as proof that someone made it through, and lived to tell the story in better days. In all my shows, movies, books, and games, I couldn't find stories about someone like me. The details and broad strokes never quite matched up with how I felt, or what I struggled with. There was no evidence that anyone like me had survived a hard time. And sometimes I wondered if, maybe, there was a reason for that.

The worst parts of my own years as an out-of-place teenager were the *Carrie*-adjacent levels of bullying and untreated mental health issues I had to endure. But the *second* worst part was feeling completely abandoned on a cosmic level when all this shit was going down.

Then I played *PaRappa*. And the game's lovingly crafted title character was close to how I saw myself. Closer than anything had come before, and closer than most things since. But the reflection of my problems wasn't as important as the solution to those problems the game offered—I gotta believe.

PaRappa the Rapper is a game about joy. It's about growing up. It's about the little challenges that we face every day. It's about artists from around the world coming together to make something new, inventing new tools and processes basically every step of the way. It's about believing that you are enough, and believing that things can be better, because *you* can be better. It's about winning without making anyone else lose, and about how life can be joyful even if you're not the very best at what you do. But most of all, it is about a teenager doing his best despite feeling out of place and unworthy in the world around him, and learning to answer his insecurity with kindness and connection.

I didn't immediately turn my life around and become a teenage beacon of good mental health and hip hop thanks to PaRappa. It took a while for the game's lessons to soak in. But *PaRappa the Rapper* was there when I needed it. It's a goofy, childish, unapologetically unique game. It believes in itself from top to bottom. It's scrappy enough to feel like it's breaking the rules, but not so flimsy to risk collapsing under the weight of its own sincerity. It's a game lacking irony or snark. It was both a mirror and a beacon for what I needed to see, and what I wished I could be.

I've gotta believe, so I will. As the Master (Onion) once said: It's all in the mind.

NOTES

All game lyrics were transcribed from in-game footage, and cross-referenced against each song's post on Genius: https://bit.ly/3NYX1pj.

The following interviews were conducted by me, and are quoted directly or paraphrased when relevant throughout this book. Some quotes were edited for clarity and concision. Sources not directly named in the final draft still helped me by sharing their time, knowledge, and insight:

- A preliminary version of this book's pitch document was shared with Rodney Greenblat in March 2020, and a video interview was conducted in January 2021.
- An email interview with Masaya Matsuura was conducted in January and February 2021, and Matsuura responded with answers in both Japanese and translated-by-him English.
- A video interview with music producer Paul Chin was conducted in January 2021.
- A phone interview was conducted with Saundra Williams in June 2021.
- A video interview with James Mielke was conducted in March 2022.

- A video interview with Leigh Alexander was conducted in April 2022.
- A video interview with Matt Boch was conducted in May 2022.
- A video interview with journalist and critic Patrick Lucas Austin was conducted in May 2022.
- A video interview with Gita Jackson was conducted in June 2022.

All remaining sources, references, or ancient GameFAQs guides are outlined below in order of appearance.

CHAPTER 1: WORTH THE WAIT

All distance/travel times are rough estimates.

CHAPTER 2: PLAYSTATION STARTUP NOISE

Jampack Vol. 2 menu details referenced via a YouTube video uploaded by Mr Demo Guy on June 12, 2020 (https://youtu.be/pDbGkrnxltI).

CHAPTER 3: THE HIP-HOP HERO

The Frank Ocean song referenced is "Start," the first track on *Channel Orange* (2012). The sample begins around 0:20.

"PaRappa The Rapper Review" was published at GameSpot on September 18, 1998 (via Internet Archive): https://bit.ly/3Gbb7Sz.

PlayStation Magazine's review of *PaRappa the Rapper* was published in Issue #002, October 1997. An Internet Archive scan of the page can be found here: https://bit.ly/3hFV84L.

Scary Larry's review of "PaRappa the Rappa" [sic] was published in *GamePro* Issue #110, November 1997. A scan of the page can be found at Internet Archive: https://bit.ly/3tsZ77m.

The GameLengths average *FF7* playtime remains the same as of November 2022: https://bit.ly/3G8u7Bb.

Chris Johnston's "Sony Awards Top PlayStation Games" was published at GameSpot on May 18, 1998 (via Internet Archive): https://bit.ly/3Twxc0T.

The 1998 PlayStation Awards winners were listed on PlayStation's official Japanese website (via Internet Archive): https://bit.ly/3hFwp0t.

CHAPTER 4: A GAME MADE BY ARTISTS

Rodney Alan Greenblat's biography and a list of his selected works and accomplishments can be found on his official website, Whimsyload (whimsyload.com): https://bit.ly/3ttPw05.

A brief MobyGames page about NanaOn-Sha (https://bit.ly/3g27PX8) was consulted in this chapter. NanaOn-Sha's official company website is no longer active as of November 12, 2022. Previous versions were built in Flash, and therefore cannot be easily accessed via the Internet Archive.

Nick Accordino published "Interview: The Untold Story of PaRappa the Rapper" at PlayStation.Blog on April 4, 2017: https://bit.ly/3UQ8fhP.

Details and basic information around *Dazzeloids*, *Tunin' Glue*, and the Bandai Pippin Atmark were verified thanks to their relevant pages on the Pippin @World & Atmark Wikipedia (https://bit.ly/3WYFEsx).

CHAPTER 5: U RAPPIN'

The Toru Iwatani/Shigeru Miyamoto anecdote has been repeated by various sources over the years. HSALS published "EXCLUSIVE: Interview with Toru Iwatani, creator of Pac-Man" at Geek Culture on May 22, 2015 (via Internet Archive: https://bit.ly/3hBgL67). It quotes Iwatani as follows: "Mr. Shigeru Miyamoto, who developed 'Super Mario Bros.' told me that the game was influenced by Namco's 'PAC-LAND'."

VME has no internet footprint to speak of outside of the *Quest for Fame* Wikipedia page that does not cite any sources (https://bit.ly/3UzAku3). *Quest for Fame*'s wiki is often confused for the wiki of a famous racehorse with the same name. All descriptions of VME's games were cross-referenced with gameplay footage on YouTube.

All details and descriptions of Bemani games come from my firsthand experience as a teenager who just really loved music games.

CHAPTER 6: IT'S ALL IN THE MIND

All Ryu Watabe quotes and information come from a translated interview posted by Shmuplations, a fan-supported archive translating and preserving interviews with Japanese game developers (via the Internet Archive): https://bit.ly/3Esnkkk. Shmupulations cites the original Japanese source as "the official strategy guide," which most likely means the *PaRappa the Rapper Official Guide Book* published by Futabasha in 1998. No comprehensive scans of the entire book exist online, and I was only able to find a single black-and-white image of a book page with Watabe and Prince Fleaswallow surrounded by Japanese text from a (now-removed) Yahoo! Japan auction. All of the major details in the interview (and many more that were new to me) were corroborated in an interview featuring Watabe on the podcast *In Conversation with ATF*, hosted by Amber the Fangirl. The episode, "In Conversation with ATF - MC RYU (Ryu Watabe)" was published on November 27, 2021 and can be found on YouTube: https://youtu.be/NeA-NufY8CA.

CHAPTER 7: JUST SITTIN' IN THE CAR

All information was provided to me by Saundra Williams during our phone interview.

CHAPTER 8: MONEY, MONEY, MONEY—IT'S ALL YOU NEED

Christopher "Lenky Don" Thomas died suddenly on January 28, 2022. I verified this through a series of Facebook posts shared by his aunt, as well as a now-closed GoFundMe campaign for funeral expenses. He was survived by his two daughters. No links to those sources are being provided both for the sake of their privacy.

CHAPTER 9: EVERY SINGLE DAY, STRESS COMES IN EVERY WAY

Michelle Lorraine Burks passed away on February 5, 2016, in her home state of Texas. This was verified through her obituary page.

One of the best things I found while researching this book isn't directly referenced anywhere, but feels important to share. A YouTube channel called Everything PaRappa uploaded "UJL + PTR - Full Concert (Live @ The Roxy 8/26/99)" on December 30, 2016 (https://youtu.be/bBEeLY5HGGU). The video is a 30-minute concert performance at an *Um Jammer Lammy* promotional event at The Roxy in New York City in August, 1999. Michelle Burks (going by "Mickey Burks"), Ryu Watabe, and Dred Foxx all share lead vocals across a selection of tracks from *Lammy* and *PaRappa*. Masaya Matsuura is on keyboards, Rodney Greenblat is in the crowd, and Sara Ramirez, the Tony Award-winning voice of Lammy, sings.

CHAPTER 10: REMIXED & REMASTERED

Kyle Orland's "Hackers find 'official,' usable PSP emulator hidden in PS4's PaRappa" was published at Ars Technica on

March 9, 2018 http://bit.ly/3kD3qvz. It both links to the original thread started by KiiWii at GBATemp and adds more context.

All technical explanations were supplied via phone interview by Matt Boch. I conducted some additional research to bolster my own understanding of the concepts they explained to me, all of which supported Boch's original examples.

Stephen Totilo's "Carmack Being Carmack: A Dozen Minutes With One of Video Game's Smartest People" was published at Kotaku on June 6, 2012 (via Internet Archive): https://bit.ly/3E6K9bR. The original, embedded video was titled "John Carmack Talks About VR," and has since been made private. YouTube channel Sandra Schlichting has re-uploaded the video, now named "Creator of Doom John Carmack shows his reality at E3 2012," on June 9, 2012 (https://youtu.be/GVDXXfbz3QE).

CHAPTER 11: PARAPPA THE RAPPER, TOO

Additional interviews I conducted with Paul Chin and Patrick Lucas Austin were very useful for this section, though not ultimately quoted.

After this chapter was written, a couple of new works came out in 2022 that explore the themes of looking for Black representation in animation. One is Jordan Calhoun's book, *Piccolo Is Black: A Memoir of Race, Religion, And Pop Culture*. Another is the eighth episode of the fourth season of *Atlanta*, "The Goof Who Sat By the Door." It is a fictional documentary about the creation of *A Goofy Movie*, and how it was designed to be "the Blackest movie of all time."

CHAPTER 12: GOOD ENOUGH

All information was provided to me by Masaya Matsuura.

CHAPTER 13: (C)RAP BATTLE

I first learned about the "Roxanne Wars" (and a good deal of the other hip hop historical facts in this book) by reading Dan Charnas's book, *The Big Payback: The History of the Business of Hip-Hop*, published by Penguin in 2011.

Natalie Weiner's "The Story of Roxanne Shanté: How a Teenager From Queens Became Rap's First Female Star" was published at Billboard on March 1, 2018 (via the Internet Archive): https://bit.ly/3fYVrHp.

CHAPTER 14: YOU GOTTA DO WHAT?

All Ryu Watabe anecdotes and quotes come from the same Shmuplations source featured above.

CHAPTER 15: TRANSLATING COOL

The GameFAQs guide for *PaRappa the Rapper*, "FAQ (PS)" by ruyeyama, was last updated to version 1.2 on December 24, 2000: https://bit.ly/3A7wlNe.

The YouTube link that Masaya Matsuura sent to me, "Swedish Child Orchestra (Hilarious!!!) - Richard Strauss - Also Sprach Zarathustra," was uploaded by the channel coloboque on October 9, 2009 (https://youtu.be/5umEUBDXfU0). Seemingly rattled by the comments they received pointing out that the actual artist was Portsmouth Sinfonia, the video description now has a brief addendum correctly attributing the source, asking people to "chillax captain," and admitting that they "can't even remember why I named the video like that 7y ago."

CHAPTER 16: I GOTTA BELIEVE!!

Douglass Perry's "Rapping With PaRappa's Maker" was published at IGN on August 28, 1999 (https://bit.ly/3trBADD), which means it was almost certainly conducted the day after The Roxy show sourced earlier in this section. The article contains the (at the time, very relevant) Ricky Martin quote from Matsuura, as well as a small moment where Greenblat politely reacts to his characters being warped through the horny, edgy lens of 90s video game advertising.

I have watched gameplay footage of the uncensored scenes from *Um Jammer Lammy*, and also talked about them directly with Rodney Greenblat.

I made exactly seven Aerosmith jokes. I'm only telling you this now because I don't want you to miss a thing.

Now it's eight.

ACKNOWLEDGMENTS

Like PaRappa, I am also deeply in love with a brilliant woman who is basically a sentient flower. Krista, thank you for your support, patience, and kindness as I brought this project to life.

Cassiopeia, you are a dog, and cannot read this. But thank you for joining the family.

I lost a parent—my Grandma—while writing this book, but my Mom lost her too. Thank you for nurturing my love of reading, and flatly believing in my future as a writer when I didn't believe in anything, least of all myself. I love you, Mom.

I also found a parent, too. Pops, thank you for being here, and for being you. It's the best thing you could possibly be.

I believed I could write a whole book sharing my thoughts about a video game because I've been sharing these thoughts my whole life with my brother, Brian. Thank you for listening, and sharpening my dull mind against your sharp one.

I am deeply grateful for everyone who added their voice and perspective to these pages. Everyone I interviewed, and all of my advance readers and editors: David Craddock and Dennis Burkett, I cannot thank you enough for your generosity and excellent taste.

A perpetual thanks goes to everyone at Boss Fight Books who, by their powers combined, have tricked the world into making me look like a competent and coherent nonfiction author. To the proofreaders, our copyeditor, and our layout and cover designers—thank you so much for bringing these words to life. I am forever grateful.

Finally: When I started this project in June 2020, I told Gabe and Mike at Boss Fight Books that my first draft should take six months to finish, tops. I am writing this sentence over two-and-a-half years later.

Thank you both for your patience in the face of my stunningly inaccurate optimism.

ALSO FROM BOSS FIGHT BOOKS